THE
HOLE
THING

Madeli
Rip

ST. JOHN'S HOSPITAL AUXILIARY

THE HOLE THING

VOLUME 1

FAVORITE RECIPES FROM JACKSON HOLE

Published by:
St. John's Hospital Auxiliary
Jackson, Wyoming

Foreword

Living in Jackson Hole is a wonder few will experience. For most, a lifetime in this valley is not enough for its beauty is unsurpassed. The warm, friendly hospitality of its citizens is as big as the "w-hole" outdoors.

This spectacular valley known as Jackson Hole was named by an early trapper, William Sublette, after his partner, Davy Jackson. Indians rendezvoused here in the summer as the hunting was superb and both French Canadians and American trappers made Jackson Hole a haven as they trapped for beaver pelts. A hole, in western parlance, refers to a valley completely surrounded by mountains, usually used by some trapper as a rendezvous spot for trading with the Indians. Our valley is edged on the East by the Gros Ventres (Grow Vont, meaning Big Belly) and the majestic Tetons form a wall on the West. The Snake River meanders through the sage brush valley where elk, moose, and deer abound.

Today, our valley attracts people from all over the world. The gorgeous scenery has brought many to live here. Spring offers fishing and bear hunting. The summer draws us out for backpacking, pack trips, and float trips down the Snake River. Fall, of course, is the hunting season and winter is glorious for skiing and snowmobiling.

Jackson Hole has several small towns, the town of Jackson being the largest. The first settlers came to Jackson Hole in 1884. Since then, the population has grown rapidly. People have moved here from all over the United States bringing with them their own customs and cuisine. Southwestern dishes, New England food, Southern cooking, and midwestern fare have all joined with the typical western food, to give us a cuisine that is both varied and delicious. From mouth watering campfire stews to gourmet meals with a continental flair, a sampling of Jackson Hole cooking has been collected in this volume for your enjoyment. Thus, we give you "The Hole Thing," and wish you a BON APPETIT!

Acknowledgments

We wish to sincerely thank the artists who have contributed so generously of their time and talents to make our book so special. Our beautiful cover was designed by the talented John Clymer who lives in Jackson Hole. Nine local artists have contributed the chapter sketches of actual scenes in our spectacular valley.

Gene Blaylock   Roy Kerswill
John Clymer   Mickey McGuire
Keith Fay   Greg McHuron
Joanne Hennes   Conrad Schwiering
            Ron Stewart

The vignettes were drawn by
Sue Everett, Madeline Rippo, Jacqueline Vashro
and Joel Zitting.

Cookbook Committee
Marge D'Atri — Chairman
Robin Lightner — Co-chairman   Beth McKee
Jennifer Clark   Judy Montgomery
Sue Everett   Jane Skeoch
Alice Glass   Ellie Wiegand

A special thanks to Tricia Bauman for her many hours of typing.

Table of Contents

Illustrations

BEGINNINGS

APPETIZERS

Antipasto

Delicious spread on crackers or as hors d'oeuvres.

Complicated

Yields: 22 pints

Preparation Time: 40 minutes
Cooking Time: 20 minutes
Process Time: 20 minutes

1 quart oil
1 quart vinegar
1 cup chopped parsley
1 cup chopped anchovies
1 quart red tomatoes (peeled)
1 can tomato paste
1 quart cubed carrots
1 quart cut green beans
1 quart yellow wax beans
1 head cauliflower (in pieces)
1 quart chopped pickled sweet
    cherry peppers

1 quart pickling onions
1 quart chopped green tomatoes
1 quart drained green olives
    (non-pimentos)
1 quart black olives
1 quart mushrooms
2 pkgs. large frozen peas
3-4 cans of tuna (6½ oz. size)
1 bottle catsup
1 quart cubed red sweet peppers
1 quart cubed green peppers

Bring oil, vinegar, parsley, anchovies, and red tomatoes, and tomato paste to a boil; add carrots, beans, cauliflower, onions and cook until nearly tender (still crunchy). Add green tomatoes, boil five minutes. Add remaining ingredients, plus seasonings to taste. Fill jars, seal and steam for 20 minutes in hot water. I cook all the ingredients in a large electric oven to prevent sticking or scorching.

Irene Brown

Artichoke Squares

This is easy with Food Processors! ! !

Average

Yield: 50 hors d'oeuvres

Preparation Time: 30 minutes
Baking Time: 30-35 minutes
Oven Temperature: 325°

2 6-oz. jars of marinated
    artichoke hearts
1 small onion, finely chopped
1 clove of garlic, minced
4 eggs
1/4 cup bread crumbs

1/4 tsp. salt
1/8 tsp. pepper
1/8 tsp. Oregano
1/2 lb. sharp Cheddar, grated
2 Tbsp. parsley, minced

Drain liquid from one jar of artichoke hearts into frying pan. Drain and discard liquid from other jar. Chop artichokes and set aside. Saute onion and garlic until limp, over medium heat. Beat eggs in mixing bowl and add bread crumbs and all seasonings; stir in cheese, parsley, artichokes and onion-garlic mixture. Pour into greased 10" square pan and bake at 325° for 30-35 minutes, or until set. Cool in pan and cut into 1" squares. Serve cool or reheat at 325° for 10-12 minutes. Do not try to cut without cooling, or squares will crumble.

Jane Skeoch

Simple Cheese Dip

Easy

Yields: 2 cups

Preparation Time: 15 minutes
Baking Time: 20 minutes
Oven Temperature: 400°

1½ lbs. processed cheese
    (Velveeta)

½ lb. bacon
1 bunch green onions

Grate cheese. Fry bacon, drain, and crumble. Chop onions finely. Mix all and place in a pretty oven-proof dish and bake at 400° for 20 minutes. May need to stir, before serving hot with crackers. Should be kept warm during serving. Tastes best with Triscuits!!

Jane Skeoch

Rotel Cheese Dip

Excellent accompaniment to your wild game dishes.

Easy   *Preparation Time: 15 minutes*
Yield: Serves 12

1 can Rotel tomatoes with   1 2-lb. pkg. of Velveeta cheese
   green chilies

In the top of a double boiler over high heat, combine the cheese and tomatoes until well blended. Place in a chafing dish and serve as a dip with tortilla or corn chips or raw vegetables.

Judy Barbour
from her book,
Elegant Elk, Delicious Deer

Linda Fleming's Hot Crab Dip

A very good, tasty dip.

Easy   *Preparation Time: 15 minutes*
                                          Baking Time: 15 minutes
Yield: 2 cups   *Oven Temperature: 375°*

1 8-oz. pkg. cream cheese   1 cup fresh crabmeat -OR-
2 Tbsp. onion, finely chopped   1 6½-oz. can crabmeat
½ tsp. creamy horseradish   1 Tbsp. milk
dash pepper   ¼ tsp. salt
½ cup sliced almonds

Blend all ingredients together except the almonds. Place in a greased 8" casserole dish. Sprinkle with almonds. Bake at 375° for 15 minutes.

This may be served with raw vegetables for dipping carrot sticks, celery sticks, broccoli and cauliflower fleurets, etc., and with crisp crackers.

Judy Barbour
Jane Skeoch

Cheese Ball

Easy
Yield: 2½ cups

Preparation Time: 10 minutes
Chilling Time: 1 hour

2 8-oz. pkgs cream cheese
1 cup pecans, finely chopped
2 Tbsp. onions, chopped
½ cup pecans, chopped
parsley

1 8-oz. can crushed pineapple
¼ cup green pepper, chopped
2 tsp. seasoned salt
maraschino cherries

Soften cream cheese gradually. Stir in well-drained crushed pineapple, 1 cup pecans, green pepper, onion and salt. Chill well. Form in ball and roll in chopped pecans. Chill until serving. Garnish with maraschino cherries and parsley. Serve with assorted crackers.

Jo Case

Macadamia Nut Cheese Ball

Easy
Yield: 2 cheeseballs

Preparation Time: 10 minutes
Chilling Time: 1 hour

2 pkgs. (8-oz.) cream cheese,
  softened
1½ cups grated Cheddar cheese
2 tsp. minced onion

½ cup chopped sweet pickles
½ cup finely chopped
  macadamia nuts

In a small bowl combine cream cheese, Cheddar cheese, onion, sweet pickles and mix well. Shape into a ball. Roll ball in chopped nuts. Cover and refrigerate several hours or until well chilled. Serve with crackers.

Judy Barbour
from her book,
Elegant Elk, Delicious Deer

Apostle Island Yacht Club Cocktail Meatballs

These can be done in advance and reheated.

Average
Yield: 50 balls

Preparation Time: 20 minutes
Simmer: 30 minutes

2 lbs. ground beef
1 can water chestnuts
⅓ cup minced onions
¾ cup bread crumbs
3 tsp. parsley -OR-
  1 tsp. dried parsley
1 can beef broth

½ cup milk
½ tsp. marjoram
¼ tsp. pepper
1½ tsp. salt
1 egg, slightly beaten
1 tsp. Worcestershire sauce
¾ cup dry white wine

Combine ground beef with onions, bread crumbs, milk, egg, and seasonings. Cut water chestnuts into quarters and form ground meat into balls enclosing a piece of water chestnut in the center of each. Brown meatballs in butter, add beef broth and wine and simmer covered for ½ hour.

Judy Montgomery

Parmesan Party Dip

Average
Yield: 2 cups

Preparation Time: 15 minutes

1 2¼-oz. jar dried beef
¼ cup chopped onion
1 Tbsp. margarine
1 cup milk

¼ cup Parmesan cheese
1 8-oz. pkg. cream cheese
2 Tbsp. chopped parsley
French bread chunks

Cut the beef into pieces. Cover with hot water and drain immediately. Saute onion in margarine. Stir in remaining ingredients, except bread. Serve hot with bread chunks—fondue style.

Lorraine Meckem

Secret Shrimp Dip

The anonymous donor was sworn to secrecy regarding the origin of this recipe.

Average
Yield: 1½ cups

Preparation Time: 10 minutes
Chilling Time: 1 hour

1 4-oz. can shrimp
1 Tbsp. shrimp broth from can
1 tsp. Worcestershire sauce
dash of pepper

1 8-oz. pkg. cream cheese
1 tsp. or more of lemon juice
1 Tbsp. mayonnaise
½ tsp. or more of onion juice

Rub mixing bowl with garlic or garlic salt. Mix all of the above together adding liquids slowly to the cream cheese in order to preserve smooth consistency. Refrigerate until about an hour before serving. This is more tasty if made a day ahead.

Cook Book Committee

Mother Brown's Shrimp Ball

Great for cocktail parties!

Easy
Serves: 10

Preparation Time: 10 minutes
Refrigeration Time: Overnight

2 cans (4½ oz.) shrimp, whole
½ cup mayonnaise
2 Tbsp. minced onions
dab of Worcestershire sauce

1 cup catsup
2 Tbsp. horseradish
2 tsp. lemon juice

Combine shrimp, mayonnaise, onion, and Worcestershire sauce. Form into a ball and refrigerate overnight (covered). Before serving, combine catsup, horseradish, and lemon juice. Spoon some of the sauce on top of ball. Serve the remainder in a separate dish to be spread on crackers or shrimp mixture.

Sue Everett

Shrimp Dip

Easy   *Preparation Time: 10 minutes*
Yield: 3 cups

1 pint mayonnaise   1 tsp. carroway seed
½ cup chopped green onions   1 cup cottage cheese
½ tsp. dry mustard   1 tsp. garlic salt
½ Tbsp. black pepper   1 Tbsp. catsup
1 tsp. celery seed   1½ Tbsp. dry sherry
3 tsp. Tabasco sauce   2 cans (4½ oz.) small shrimp

Mix all ingredients together. Refrigerate. Serve with Triscuit crackers.

Rosemary Laumeyer

Crab & Avocado Cocktail with Louis Dressing

This is the all-time favorite appetizer of our gourmet dinner group.

Easy   *Preparation Time: 30 minutes*
Serves: 12

3 large avocados, peeled and   DRESSING:
  cubed
2½ lbs. cooked lump crabmeat,   1 cup mayonnaise
  blue or king crab   ¼ cup chili sauce
½ cup celery, finely chopped   1 Tbsp. chopped onion
½ cup radish slices   1 Tbsp. chives
¼ cup lemon juice   2 Tbsp. parsley, chopped
½ cup vinegar   ¼ cup whipping cream, whipped
3 Tbsp. olive oil
2 Tbsp. chopped shallots
¼ tsp. cayenne

Combine avocado cubes with crabmeat, celery, radishes, lemon juice, vinegar, olive oil, shallots, cayenne, and salt to taste. Mound on serving dish surrounded by lettuce, tomato quarters and lemon slices. Top with dressing.

DRESSING: Combine mayonnaise, parsley, chili sauce, onion and chives. Mix well. Fold in whipped cream and a dash of cayenne.

Judy Montgomery

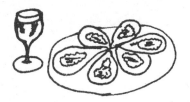

Oysters and Artichokes

This dish requires a lengthy preparation, but it can be done the night before.

Complicated

Serves: 8

Preparation Time: 2½ hours
Baking Time: 15-20 minutes
Oven Temperature: 350°

5 artichokes, boiled
1½ pints oysters (3 doz.)
2 cups water
2 sticks butter
½ cup flour
1¾ cups finely chopped onion
9 cloves garlic, minced

1 tsp. thyme
2 tsp. salt
½ tsp. lemon juice
¼ cup chopped parsley
bread crumbs
8 thin slices lemon
Garnish: finely chopped parsley

Remove leaves from boiled artichokes, saving some nice firm ones to use as decoration and dippers. Scrape the remaining leaves and reserve the pulp. Cut artichoke bottoms into eighths and place in ramekins. Drain oysters, reserving liquor. Soak oysters in 2 cups water for 30 minutes. Drain, reserving liquor. Make a dark brown roux with butter and flour; add onions and garlic. Saute until tender (about 20 minutes). Add thyme, salt, pepper, artichoke pulp, and lemon juice. Slowly stir in oyster liquor, approximately 1½ cups. The gravy should be very thick. Simmer slowly for 45 minutes stirring occasionally. Add oysters and parsley. Cook 10 minutes. Remove from heat and spoon into ramekins and refrigerate. When ready to reheat, sprinkle with bread crumbs, top with lemon slices, and thoroughly heat in a 350° oven. Garnish with chopped parsley and surround ramekins with artichoke leaves. If you wish to serve more than eight, simply add a few more artichokes.

Marilynn Mullikin

Crab-Meat Mold

An excellent and unusual spread.

Average	*Preparation Time: 20 minutes*
Yield: 1½ quart mold	*Chilling Time: 6 hours*

1 can (10¾ oz.) shrimp or
  mushroom soup, undiluted
2 pkgs. (3 oz. size) cream cheese
1 cup mayonnaise
1 cup cold water

1 cup finely chopped celery
¼ cup finely chopped onion
2 envelopes unflavored gelatin
7½ oz. crabmeat, drained
  and flaked

In medium saucepan, combine soup, cheese, and onion. Heat until cheese melts, stirring. Blend in mayonnaise and remove from heat.

In another saucepan, sprinkle gelatin over water. Over low heat, stir until gelatin dissolves. Stir in soup mixture, add crab and celery. Pour into mold for six hours or until firm. Unmold on a large platter and surround with crackers and knife for spreading.

Jo Case

Curried Ham Dip

This dip was our traditional start for Thanksgiving and Christmas dinners.

Easy	*Preparation Time: 25 minutes.*
Yield: 1 cup	

1 2½-oz. can Underwoods
  deviled ham
1 finely chopped hardboiled egg
½ tsp. curry powder

2 Tbsp. mayonnaise
2 Tbsp. sour cream
salt and pepper to taste

Combine all the ingredients. Salt and pepper to taste. Chill before serving. Serve with tortilla chips or crackers.

Marge D'Atri

Roasted Nuts

Easy

Yields: 1 cup

Preparation Time: 10 minutes
Baking Time: 10-15 minutes
Oven Temperature: 350°

1 cup nuts
  (You can use pumpkin, raw
  peanuts, sesame seeds, pumpkin
  seeds, etc.)

1 tsp. oil

INDIAN:

1/8 tsp. garlic, -OR-
  ½ tsp. garlic salt and dill -OR-
  ¼ tsp. garlic and paprika

1 tsp. curry powder
½ tsp. salt

ORIENTAL:

1 tsp. salad oil
1 tsp. sesame oil

1 tsp. sansho (Japanese pepper)
½ tsp. Chinese spice salt

SMOKEY:

¼ tsp. flavored salt
onion

1/8 tsp. garlic
savory leaves and cayenne

Spread nuts on single layer cookie sheet and bake at 350°
till golden brown, adding 1 to 2 tsp. oil and "seasonings." Stir
and shift nuts while baking.

Jill Marmelzat

SOUPS

Bean Pot Soup

Truly a meal in one soup bowl.

Average
Yield: 4 quarts

Preparation Time: Overnight
Cooking Time: 3 to 4 hours

2 cups dry pinto beans
1 lb. ham, cubed
1 quart water
2 (13½ oz. each) cans tomato juice
4 cups chicken stock
1 medium onion
3 medium garlic cloves, minced
3 Tbsp. chopped parsley
¼ cup chopped green pepper
4 Tbsp. brown sugar
1 Tbsp chili powder
1 tsp. salt

1 tsp. crushed bay leaves
1 tsp. oregano
½ tsp. ground cumin
½ tsp. rosemary
½ tsp. celery seed
½ tsp. thyme
½ tsp. marjoram
½ tsp. sweet basil
¼ tsp. curry powder
4 whole cloves
1 cup sherry

Soak beans overnight. Drain. Add remaining ingredients except sherry. Bring to a boil, reduce heat and simmer covered until beans are tender—3 to 4 hours. Add sherry and reheat to serving temperature. This freezes nicely if there is any left over.

Irene Brown

Beautiful Zucchini Soup

Really super and very low calorie.

Easy   *Preparation Time: 10 minutes*
Serves: 4   *Cooking Time: 6 minutes*

3 cups water   2 lbs. sliced small zucchini
4 chicken bouillon cubes   ¼ tsp. salt
¾ cup sliced green onion

Bring water, bouillon cubes and salt to a boil—OR use 3 cups canned or fresh chicken bouillion. Add the green onions and sliced zucchini. Boil until barely tender, about three minutes. Cool slightly in blender or food processor. Reheat and serve. Overcooking spoils the lovely green color. If you like, you may shred the zucchini instead of slicing them. Then omit the blender.

Anne Dankert

Broccoli Soup

Average   *Preparation Time: 1 hour*
Serves: 8

1 large head broccoli   2 cans Cream of Chicken Soup
1 to 2 medium onions, chopped   ½ cube butter
3 to 4 stalks celery, chopped   1 cup milk

Saute onion and celery in butter until tender and transparent. Remove with a slotted spoon leaving butter in pan. Add the Cream of Chicken Soup and enough milk to make it creamy. In the meantime, chop up broccoli in food processor or blender and add to the other ingredients. Simmer and stir constantly until broccoli is tender crisp. Or put in double boiler and simmer, stirring occasionally.

Grace Berg

Cabbage-Potato Soup

We love this, so we make a large recipe. You may wish to cut it in half.

Average   Preparation Time: 1 hour
Yield: 5 quarts

3½ quarts water, salted
8 large potatoes, diced
2 heads cabbage (green)
¼ lb. bacon (or leftover ham)
3 Tbsp. bacon fat or whatever
   drains from above

2 onions, diced or chopped
3 Tbsp (heaping) flour
1 large carton sour cream
16 oz. tomato juice
salt and pepper to taste

Cook potatoes and cabbage in salted water. In meantime, saute bacon or cook in microwave—reserve fat. Cut bacon into bits and set aside. Saute onions in bacon fat. Add flour and brown lightly. Add tomato juice and mix, then add sour cream slowly and mix up. Add above to cooked potatoes and cabbage (do not pour off water). Add bacon bits. Simmer about 5 minutes. Salt and pepper to taste.

Wynne Gensey

Clam Bisque

Average   Preparation Time: 30 minutes
Serves: 8

1 large onion, chopped (1 cup)
6 Tbsp. butter or margarine
   (¾ stick)
6 Tbsp. flour
3 8-oz. cans minced clams
   and liquid

2 8-oz. bottles clam juice
3 cups light cream or table cream
3 Tbsp. tomato paste
3 Tbsp. lemon juice

Saute onion until soft in butter in large saucepan. Stir in flour, cook, stirring constantly, until bubbly. Stir in clams and liquid and clam juice; continue cooking and stirring until mixture thickens and boils one minute. Simmer 15 minutes. Blend cream, tomato paste, and lemon juice. Heat slowly, just until hot.

Marian T. Spalding

Clam-Mushroom Bisque

Easy   *Preparation Time: 20 minutes*
Serves: 4

½ lb. (or more) fresh mushrooms   2½ cups clam broth (from cans of
2 to 4 Tbsp. butter   minced clams, add chicken
2 Tbsp. flour   broth to equal 2½ cups)
3 cans minced clams   parsley
2 cartons whipping cream   salt and pepper

Saute mushrooms in butter, stir in flour. Stir in broth and simmer 5 minutes. Heat cream, but do not boil. Add cream and drained minced clams. Add salt and pepper to taste, and add parsley.

Wynne Gensey

Cream of Chicken Soup

I served this at a Parent Meeting and they all asked for the recipe.

Average   *Preparation Time: Approx. 1 hour*
Serves: 4

1 pint of chicken stock, canned   ½ lb. fresh mushrooms (optional)
½ stick of butter   ¼ cup sour cream
¼ cup flour   salt and pepper to taste
1 pint light cream   parsley flakes for garnish
1 chicken breast, cooked and
   chopped

Melt butter in pan. Blend in flour and add chicken stock. Add all but ½ cup of cream. Cook slowly, stirring often. If you want to use mushrooms, clean and chop finely. Add to soup at this point. Add chopped chicken. Blend well. When soup has thickened, mix sour cream and remaining ½ cup of cream together. Stir into soup and simmer for five minutes. Add salt and pepper to taste and sprinkle parsley flakes on top.

Robin Lightner

Sausage and Bean Soup

This is a real good cold weather supper type dish.

Easy   *Preparation Time: 35 minutes*
Serves: 10 to 12   *Cooking Time: 40 minutes*

2 Tbsp. olive or salad oil
2 medium sized onions, chopped
2 large cloves garlic, minced or
   pressed
4 stalks celery, thinly sliced
2 medium carrots, thinly sliced
1 tsp. dry basil and oregano
3 medium-sized zucchini, cut into
   ¼ inch slices

1 lb. Italian or garlic sausage or
   Kielbasa, cut into ¼ inch
   lengths or slices
1½ quarts water
6 beef bouillon cubes
1 28-oz. can tomatoes
6 cups cooked or canned Great
   Northern beans or garbanzos,
   drained
salt and pepper to taste

In a 6 to 8 quart Dutch oven, heat oil over medium heat. Add sausage, onion, garlic and cook, stirring until the sausage begins to brown. Add celery and carrots, 1½ quarts water, bouillon cubes, tomatoes, including the liquid from tomatoes, break up tomatoes with spoon, beans, basil and oregano. Simmer covered for 20 minutes. Skim off any excess fat. This much can be done ahead. Bring soup to simmering adding more water if needed. Stir in zucchini and cook until tender, about ten minutes.

Freida Chase

EGGS AND CHEESE

All in one Brunch Egg Casserole

This is good to have for breakfast when you have company!!

Average

Serves: 6

Preparation Time: 15 minutes
Baking Time: 55-60 minutes
Oven Temperature: 325°

2 cups plain croutons
1 cup (4 oz.) Cheddar cheese,
   shredded
4 slightly beaten eggs
2 cups milk

½ tsp. salt
½ tsp. prepared mustard
1/8 tsp. onion powder
dash of pepper
4 slices of bacon

In bottom of greased 10 x 6 x 1 ¾" baking dish, combine croutons and Cheddar cheese. Combine eggs, milk, salt, mustard, onion powder, and pepper; mix till blended. Pour liquid over crouton mixture in casserole. Cook 4 slices of bacon till crisp. Drain and crumble on top of casserole. Bake 55-60 minutes in 325° oven. If everyone is not ready to eat at the same time, this can stay in oven on warm.

Jo Case

Cheese & Egg Casserole

Easy

Serves: 4

Preparation Time: 10 minutes
Baking Time: 30-40 minutes
Oven Temperature: 350°

1 pint milk
8 slices of toasted, buttered
   bread or stale bread
dash of Worcestershire Sauce

½ lb. American cheese -OR-
   Cheddar cheese
4 eggs
salt to taste

Cube bread. Grate cheese. Layer in baking dish: first bread, then cheese. Beat milk and eggs thoroughly. Pour over bread and cheese. Bake at 350° until set and brown on top.

Alice Glass

Chilequiles

This makes a good Sunday night supper with a green salad and garlic bread or use it for brunch.

Easy
Serves: 4

Preparation Time: 25 minutes

5 corn tortillas, torn in pieces
2 cups canned or fresh tomatoes
½ cup chopped onion
¼ cup chopped green pepper -OR-
   2 Tbsp. Ortega diced green chilies

½ cup sliced green onion
6 beaten eggs
½ lb. yellow cheese, cubed

Fry tortilla pieces in hot oil until crisp. Remove and pour all but one Tbsp. of the oil from the skillet. Saute chopped onion and green pepper until limp. Add tomatoes and green onion (and diced chili, if desired) and heat to boiling. Add tortilla chips and cheese. Pour over beaten eggs. Do not stir but cook gently until eggs begin to set. Then turn with a spoon until eggs are done. Serve at once.

Marge D'Atri

Chilies Rellenos

Average

Serves: 6 to 8

Preparation Time: 30 minutes
Baking Time: 30 to 45 minutes
Oven Temperature: 350°

8 egg yolks
12 egg whites
1½ cup milk
4 Tbsp. flour

2 cups Monterey Jack cheese
4 Tbsp. butter
1 large can whole green chilies

Make a white sauce with butter, flour, and milk. Cook stirring constantly over medium heat. Cool slightly and add yolks one at a time, beating rapidly. Beat egg whites until stiff. Fold in thickened sauce. Line a buttered 9 x 13 pan with sliced opened and cleaned chilies. Put a layer of cheese over chilies. Add another layer of chilies and then more cheese. Make as many layers as you like. Pour sauce mixture over chilies and cheese. Bake at 350° for 30 to 45 minutes until top is golden brown and mixture is set.

Susie Von Gontard

Eggs Benedict

Average
Serves: 4

Preparation Time: 20 minutes

4 slices Canadian bacon
2 English muffins
butter

4 eggs
Hollandaise Sauce (page 91)
dash of cayenne pepper or paprika

Fry bacon; drain on paper towels. Split muffins and toast. Butter muffins. Meanwhile poach eggs. Four minutes low altitude; Five to six minutes high altitidue. Arrange muffins on plate; top with bacon, then poached eggs. Spoon Hollandaise Sauce over eggs. Sprinkle with cayenne pepper or paprika for color. Serve hot.

Accompany with fresh fruit such as cubes of cantalope, honeydew, strawberries, green grapes or a combination of all. Additional muffins with your favorite jam will give you a sweet touch.

Robin Lightner

Green Enchilada Casserole

Average

Serves: 4

Preparation Time: 30 minutes
Baking Time: 40 minutes
Oven Temperature: 350°

1 dozen tortillas
1 cup grated Cheddar cheese
1 4-oz. can chopped green chilies
½ cup onions, chopped

1 cup canned milk
1 can cream of chicken soup -OR-
   1 can mushroom soup

Fry tortillas one at a time in oil until limp (about 10 seconds on each side). Mix the soup, milk and chilies and heat. Put one layer of tortillas in bottom of a greased casserole. Sprinkle with some onion, cheese, and some of the soup mix. Continue layering tortillas, onion, cheese, and soup. Casserole should be at least two tortillas deep. Put cheese on the top of last layer. Bake at 350°, uncovered, for 30 to 40 minutes.

Blendine Walters

Quiche Lorraine

Average

Serves: 6 to 8

Preparation Time: 30 minutes
Cooking Time: 45 minutes
Oven Temperature: 425° to 300°

1 9" unbaked pie shell
2 cups grated Swiss cheese
½ cup minced onion
6 slices bacon, fried and
   crumbled

4 eggs
1 tsp. salt
½ tsp. sugar
1/8 tsp. cayenne pepper
2 cups whipping cream

Spread onion, crumbled bacon, and cheese over pie shell. Beat eggs slightly. Add whipping cream and other ingredients and blend. Pour mixture into pie shell over onion, bacon and cheese. Bake at 425° for 15 minutes. Lower oven temperature to 300° and bake 30 minutes longer or until a knife inserted near edge comes out clean. Let stand for 10 minutes before serving. Aged cream, almost ready to turn, seems to cook faster and taste better than fresh whipping cream.

Kathy Fields

Sausage Casserole

This is a very good brunch dish or also handy to prepare ahead when you know that you will have company at breakfast time.

Easy

Serves: 4

Preparation Time: 20 minutes
Chilling Time: Overnight
Baking Time: 50 minutes
Oven Temperature: 350°

1 lb. sausage, country style
1¾ cups milk
4 slices of bread
¼ tsp. pepper
¼ tsp. dry mustard

4 eggs
¼ lb. sharp Cheddar cheese, grated
½ tsp. salt
Worcestershire sauce

Cube the four slices of bread, place in greased two quart casserole with the ¼ pound of cheese, and the sausage, browned. Beat together the one and three-fourths cup of milk, the eggs, ½ teaspoon of salt, ¼ teaspoon of pepper, ¼ teaspoon of dry mustard, and a few dashes of Worcestershire sauce. Pour the egg mixture over the sausage mixture. Cover and refrigerate for twelve hours or longer if needed. I have kept it in the refrigerator three days before cooking. When ready to use, bake covered 50 minutes at 350°.

Fern K. Nelson

Deviled Eggs

Easy
Yield: 16 halves

Preparation Time: 20 minutes

8 hard boiled eggs
1 2¼-oz. can deviled ham
2 green onions, minced
½ tsp. prepared mustard
2 Tbsp. pickle relish, sweet

salt
pepper
mayonnaise
paprika

Cut eggs in half and remove yolks. Mash yolks with fork. Add remaining ingredients except mayonnaise and paprika. Add enough mayonnaise to make mixture gooey but not runny. Fill egg whites. Sprinkle with paprika.

Robin Lightner

Sour Cream Tortilla Casserole

Average

Serves: 10 to 12

Preparation Time: 45 minutes
Baking Time: 30 minutes
Oven Temperature: 325°

½ cup chopped onion
2 Tbsp. oil
1 1-lb., 12 oz. can tomatoes
1 pkg. Lawry Taco Seasoning Mix
2 Tbsp. salsa jalapeno
12 corn tortillas

¾ cup chopped onion
1 lb. Monterey Jack cheese,
   grated
2 cups sour cream
1 tsp. seasoned salt
pepper

Saute ½ cup chopped onion in two tablespoons of oil until soft. Add tomatoes, taco seasoning mix and salsa, simmer for 15 to 20 minutes. Fry tortillas in small amount of oil, do not let crisp. Put ½ cup sauce in bottom of 13 x 9 x 2" baking dish. Put layer of tortillas over sauce and top with ⅓ of the remaining sauce, ¼ cup chopped onion, and ⅓ of the grated cheese. Repeat, making three layers of tortillas, combine sour cream, seasoned salt and pepper. Spread over the top and bake at 325° for 25 to 30 minutes. Freeze the leftovers. They can be reheated in a microwave oven, or for 15 minutes in a 350° oven.

Judy Montgomery

Scrambled Eggs with Chipped Beef

Easy

Serves: 4

Preparation Time: 5 minutes
Cooking Time: 5 minutes

8 eggs
1 3-oz. pkg. wafer sliced beef

salt and pepper
2 Tbsp. butter

Break eggs in bowl. Add salt and pepper. Beat lightly with a fork. Cut beef into bite-size pieces and add to eggs. Melt butter in skillet and add eggs to hot skillet. Scramble. Serve on toast.

Robin Lightner

Stuffed French Rolls

These can be frozen and later thawed and reheated!!

Average

Yield: 12 rolls

Preparation Time: 15 minutes
Baking Time: 20 to 30 minutes
Oven Temperature: 300°

12 sour dough French rolls
½ cup chopped olives
½ tsp. sugar
½ cup oil
¾ cup (1 lb.) extra sharp cheese, grated

1 cup tomato sauce
2 chopped hard boiled eggs
3 to 5 chopped green onion stalks
3 tsp. vinegar
½ tsp. seasoned salt

Mix all ingredients, except rolls. Slice tops off rolls, about ¼ inch or so. Scoop out center of rolls leaving generous cavity to fill. Add cheese mixture. Fill below top of the roll as ingredients melt and expand somewhat. Bake at 300° 20 to 30 minutes till center is melted and rolls are browned. During the last 4 to 5 minutes put tops on rolls to brown. Serve hot as lunch or dinner treats.

Jill Marmelzat

One-Eyed Egyptians

Easy
Serves: 4

Preparation Time: 10 minutes
Cooking Time: 10 minutes

4 eggs
butter

4 slices of bread
salt and pepper

With a cookie cutter, cut a hole in the center of each slice of bread. Hole should be slightly larger than the yolk of an egg. Heat a skillet with plenty of butter in it. Add the bread slice and fry until just beginning to turn golden. Add one egg to the center of each slice and fry until almost set. Turn and fry the other side until egg is done to your liking. Fry the "holes" at the same time and serve with the eggs.

Marge D'Atri

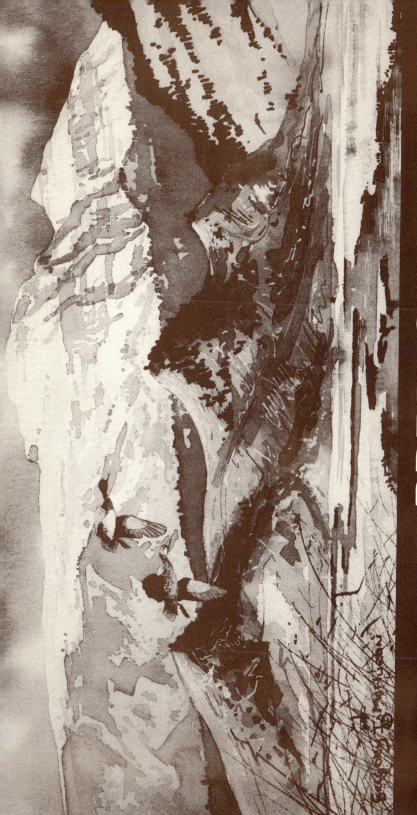

BREADS

BREADS

Basic Sweet Dough

Average   *Preparation Time: 1½ hours*

¾ cup milk   ⅓ cup warm water (105° to 115°)
½ cup sugar   2 pkgs. active dry yeast
1¼ tsp salt   3 eggs, room temperature
½ cup butter   5½ to 6½ cups of flour

Scald milk; stir in sugar, salt, and butter. Cool to 115°. Pour warm water into bowl. Sprinkle in yeast and stir until dissolved. Add milk mixture and ½ of the flour. Beat, add a little more flour, kneading until all flour is used up. Place in greased bowl turning to grease top. Cover and let rise till double. Punch down and divide for rolls, coffe cakes, etc.

Robin Lightner

Hot Cross Buns

Average   *Preparation Time: 1½ hours*
                                             Baking Time: 15 minutes
Yield: 24 buns   *Oven Temperature: 375°*

1 Basic Sweet Dough Recipe   1 cup raisins or currants
powdered sugar icing

Add raisins to dough after adding flour. Finish making dough. Divide dough and separate each half into twelve balls. Place each ball on a greased cookie sheet about four inches apart. Cover and let rise until double. Snip cross on top. Brush with slightly beaten egg whites and bake at 375° for about 15 minutes. Cool slightly and top cross with icing.

ICING:

1 egg white   a little water
powdered sugar

Mix until smooth and thick but still pours.

Robin Lightner

34

Molasses Skillet Bread

My Grandmother's recipe from Sweden. It takes a while to make, but it's worth it!!

Complicated

Yield: One 8" round bread

Preparation Time: 20 minutes
Rising Time: 2 hours
Baking Time: 45 minutes
Oven Temperature: 350°

1 pkg. dry yeast
¼ cup lukewarm water
⅔ cup scalded milk
¼ cup sugar
1 tsp. salt
¼ cup butter
¼ cup light molasses

3¼ to 3¾ cups flour
1 egg, beaten
1 cup quick or old-fashioned
oats, uncooked
GLAZE:
¼ cup honey
¼ cup oleo or butter

Soften yeast in lukewarm water. Pour scalded milk over sugar, salt, butter, and molasses. Stir to dissolve butter. Cool to lukewarm. Stir in 1 cup flour and the egg. Add softened yeast and oats. Stir in enough additional flour to make soft dough. Turn out on lightly floured board or canvas. Knead until smooth. Round dough into a ball, place in greased bowl. Brush lightly with melted butter, cover and let rise in warm place until double in size (about 1 hour). Punch down dough; cover, let rise 10 minutes. Turn onto lightly floured board. Roll into two 23" x 6" rectangles; cut into half lengthwise. Pinch lengthwise edges of each strip together to make two 23" ropes. Place one rope of dough around outside edge of a buttered 8" cast iron skillet. Wind second rope into a coil in the center of the skillet. Pinch together the ends of the two ropes where they meet. Brush lightly with butter, cover, let rise in warm place until nearly doubled in size (about 45 minutes). Bake at 350° for 30 minutes. Beat honey and butter. Brush ½ glaze on bread. Bake 15 minutes. Brush with remaining glaze, cool 10 minutes, and serve warm.

Sue Everetts

Bagels

Average

Yield: 48

Preparation Time: 2 hours
Baking Time: 30 to 35 minutes
Oven Temperature: 350°

8 pkgs. active dry yeast
17 to 18 cups sifted flour
6 cups lukewarm water
¾ cup sugar

4 Tbsp. salt
1 gallon water
1 Tbsp. sugar

In large mixer bowl, combine yeast and 7 cups flour. Combine water, sugar, and salt. Add yeast mixture. Beat at low speed ½ minute, scraping sides of bowl constantly. Beat 3 minutes at high speed. By hand, stir in enough remaining flour to make a moderately stiff dough. Turn out on lightly floured surface—knead 5 to 8 minutes. Cut into 48 portions. Smooth each portion into a ball. Punch a hole in center of each ball with floured finger. Pull gently to enlarge hole. Cover, let rise 20 minutes. In a kettle, combine 1 gallon of water and 1 Tbsp. of sugar. Bring to boil. Reduce heat to simmer. Cook 4 to 5 bagels at a time for 7 minutes, turning once. Drain. Place on ungreased baking sheet. Bake bagels at 375⁰ for 30 to 35 minutes. Makes 48.

Sandy Bommer

Sourdough Pancakes

Easy
Yield: 15 pancakes

Preparation Time: 15 minutes

1 cup sourdough starter (page 37)
1 cup flour
1 cup water or milk
½ tsp. salt

1 Tbsp. sugar
1 tsp. soda
1 egg
1½ Tbsp. cooking oil

Stir all the ingredients together and allow to rise for ten minutes. Fry on a hot griddle.

Fern Nelson

Cornbread

My daughter used this recipe for her 4-H fair exhibit and received a purple ribbon at the State Fair.

Easy   *Preparation Time: 15 minutes*
                                          Baking Time: 20 minutes
Yield: One 8" x 8" pan   *Oven Temperature: 400°*

1 8-oz. carton of plain yogurt   1 cup cornmeal
¼ cup vegetable oil   ¼ cup sugar
1 egg   ½ tsp. baking soda
1 cup flour   ½ tsp. salt

Sift dry ingredients together into a medium-sized bowl. In a small bowl, beat egg; add yogurt and vegetable oil. Mix. Add egg mixture to dry ingredients. Stir just until dry ingredients are dampened. Mixture will be lumpy. Do not overmix. Pour into a 8" x 8" square, greased baking pan. Bake at 400° for 20 minutes.

Carol McCain

Sourdough Start

Easy   *Preparation Time: 10 minutes*
Yield: 3 cups   *Fermenting Time: About 3 days*

1 cup plain yogurt   1 tsp. dry yeast (if necessary)
1 cup flour

Place one cup of plain yogurt in a quart glass, ceramic or earthen jar, stir in one cup flour, beating to a smooth paste. Cover the jar and place in a warm spot for two days. Uncover and look at the mixture. If bubbles are showing, it means the start has acquired yeast bacteria from the air. If so, it can work for another day (until it is good and bubbly) before being used in a batter or stored in the refrigerator. If no bubbles have started in the two-day time, it may be well to give it a teaspoonful of granulated dry, or compressed yeast. Just stir it in and give it another twelve hours to work. (Each time you use the sourdough take out ½ cup starter first.) Mix two cups flour and one cup water into starter twelve hours before you want to use the sourdough next. Leave it out in a warm place to work.

Fern K. Nelson

Dilly Bread

Super good—freezes well.

Average

Serves: 8 to 10, 1 round loaf

Preparation Time: 20 minutes
Rising Times: 1st 50 to 60 minutes
2nd 30 to 40 minutes
Baking Time: 40 to 50 minutes

1 pkg. active dry yeast
¼ cup warm water
1 cup creamed cottage cheese,
   heated to lukewarm
2 Tbsp. sugar
1 tsp. salt

1 Tbsp. onion, minced
1 Tbsp. butter
2 tsp. dill seed
¼ tsp. soda
1 egg, unbeaten
2¼ to 2½ cups all-purpose flour

Soften yeast in water. Combine in mixing bowl; cottage cheese, sugar, onion, butter, dill seed, salt, soda, egg, and softened yeast. Add flour to form stiff dough. Beat well after each addition. Cover. Let rise in warm place (85 to 95 degrees) until light and double in size (50 to 60 minutes). Stir dough down. Turn into well greased 8 inch round 1½ to 2 quart casserole. Let rise in warm place until light (30 to 40 minutes). Bake at 350° 40 to 50 minutes until golden brown. Brush with melted butter and sprinkle with salt.

Susie Carlson

One Hour Yeast Rolls

A good roll if you want yeast rolls at the last minute.

Easy

Yield: 3 dozen

Preparation Time: 40 minutes
Baking Time: 20 minutes
Oven Temperature: 400°

2 yeast cakes
1½ cups warm buttermilk
¼ cup warm water
4½ cups flour

3 Tbsp. sugar
½ tsp. soda
½ cup melted butter
1 tsp. salt

Beat all the ingredients together until smooth. Let rise ten minutes. Roll out. Shape, then let rise thirty minutes. Bake at 400° for twenty minutes.

Blendine Walters

Maple Syrup Brown Bread

Average

Yield: 2 loaves

Rising Time: 3 hours
Baking Time: 40 to 45 minutes
Oven Temperature: 375°

¾ cup uncooked rolled oats
1¼ cups boiling water
1 pkg. dry yeast
¼ cup warm water (105° to 115°)
½ cup milk
⅓ cup pure maple syrup
¼ cup granulated sugar

¼ cup butter
2 tsp. salt
5 cups all-purpose flour
½ cup golden raisins
pure maple or maple blended
  syrup
maple or dark brown sugar

Combine oats and 1¼ cups water in small bowl. Cover. Let stand until water is absorbed; about 20 minutes. Meanwhile, dissolve yeast in warm water in large bowl; let stand until bubbly, about 5 minutes. Combine milk, ⅓ cup syrup, sugar, butter, and salt in small saucepan. Heat over low heat until butter is melted. Cool to lukewarm. Stir into yeast. Stir in oat mixture. Mix in flour and raisins to make a stiff dough. Turn dough onto lightly floured surface. Knead until smooth and elastic, about 10 minutes. Place in greased bowl. Turn greased side up and cover with towel. Let rise in warm place until double, about 1½ hours. (Dough is ready if finger impression remains.) Punch dough down. Divide in half. Roll each half into a rectangle 16" x 8". Roll up, beginning at short edge. Pinch ends together to seal. Place seam side down in 2 greased loaf pans 8½ x 4½ x 2½". Cover, let rise until double, about 1½ hours. Heat oven 375°. Bake 40 to 45 minutes. Cool in pans 10 minutes. Remove. Brush tops with maple syrup and sprinkle with maple sugar.

Helen Green

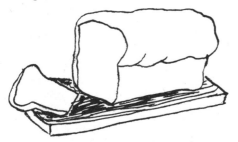

Feather-Light Rolls

Average

Preparation Time: 30 minutes
Rising Time: Overnight, plus 6 hours
Baking Time: 20 minutes

Yield: 32 rolls

Oven Temperature: 375°

1 pkg. dry yeast
¼ cup water
1 Tbsp. sugar
1 cup scalded milk
½ cup sugar

½ cup melted butter
¾ tsp. salt
3 eggs, well beaten
3¼ to 4 cups flour, sifted
melted butter

Proof yeast in 1 Tbsp. sugar and ½ cup water. Add cooled milk, ½ cup sugar, butter, salt and eggs to yeast mixture. Mix, add 2 cups flour and beat until smooth. Add remaining flour and knead for about 10 minutes. The dough may require more or less flour but should not be stiff. Cover and let rise 5 to 6 hours. Can be made the night before and refrigerated or left in a cool place. Knead dough a little. Roll out in desired shape. Use butter generously on tops!! Let rise 4 to 6 hours. Bake at moderate temperature, 375°, for about 20 minutes.

Lorraine Meckem

Pumpkin Bread

GREAT!!

Average

Preparation Time: 20 minutes
Cooking Time: 65 to 75 minutes

Yield: 9" x 3" loaf

Oven Temperature: 350°

1 cup sugar
½ cup brown sugar
1 cup pumpkin
½ cup salad oil
2 eggs
2 cups flour
1 tsp. soda

½ tsp. salt
¼ tsp. nutmeg
½ tsp. cinnamon
¼ tsp. ginger
1 cup raisins
½ cup nuts
¼ cup water

Combine sugars, pumpkin, salad oil and eggs. Beat until blended. Add flour, and seasonings. Beat well. Stir in raisins, nuts and water. Put in a well greased loaf pan. Bake at 350° for 65 to 75 minutes.

Judy Lowder

Whole Wheat Buttermilk Bread

Very good!! Keep dough on soft, sticky side.

Average

Preparation Time: 30 minutes
Rising Time: 2½ hours
Baking Time: 30 to 40 minutes

Yield: 4 large loaves

Oven Temperature: 400°

2 cups warm water
3 pkgs. dry yeast
2 cups warm water
2 Tbsp. salt
½ cup oil
¾ cup honey

1 cup powdered buttermilk
9 cups (about) unsifted whole
   wheat flour
3 cups white flour
1 to 2 eggs
1 cup plain yogurt

Dissolve yeast in first 2 cups warm water. In large mixing bowl, combine the second 2 cups warm water with salt, oil, honey, buttermilk, and yogurt. Add one or two eggs, slightly beaten. Add 4 cups whole wheat flour and beat well with mixer at medium speed for 4 to 5 minutes. Stir in yeast mixture. Add 3 cups white flour and 1 cup whole wheat flour. Stir in remaining flour until you can no longer stir or beat. Then pour on counter and add remaining flour by kneading it for 15 minutes. DO NOT GET DOUGH TOO STIFF!! Depending on weather, you may use only 8 cups of flour. Place in greased bowl. Cover and let rise in warm place until double (about 1½ hours). Knead down. Cover and let rise again, until doubled. Punch down dough and let rest on board for 15 to 20 minutes. Divide into 4 equal parts. Shape into loaves and place in 4 large greased bread tins. Cover and let rise until double in bulk in warm place. Bake at 450° for 30 to 40 minutes.

Lee Jensen

Ice Box Whole Wheat and Bran Muffins

Great!!

Average

Yield: 64 muffins

Preparation Time: 30 minutes
Baking Time: 20 minutes
Oven Temperature: 375°

2 cups 100% (Nabisco) bran
2 cups boiling water
1 cup shortening
1½ cups white sugar
1 cup brown sugar
4 eggs
1 quart buttermilk

2 cups whole wheat flour
3 cups white flour
5 tsp. soda
1 tsp. salt
4 cups "All Bran" long shredded
    cereal

Pour boiling water over bran (Nabisco) and cool. Cream shortening and sugar. Add eggs and beat well with mixer until blended. Add buttermilk. Stir in soaked bran mixture. Add whole wheat flour unsifted (spoon into cup). Sift white flour with soda and salt and add to above mixture. Beat on medium speed for a couple minutes. Stir in "All Bran." Batter may be fairly thick and makes 1 gallon. (Spoon or pour into another container the amount you wish to retain and bake another time.) Add 1 cup raisins, nuts, berries, dates or whatever you wish. Spoon into greased and floured muffin tins, filling ¾ full. Bake 15 to 20 minutes at 375⁰. This batter can be stored in a glass or ceramic container in refrigerator for as long as a month, and then whenever you desire muffins, take out the amount you need.

Lee Jensen

Rhubarb Preserves

Easy
Yield: 1 quart

Preparation Time: 2½ to 3 hours
Cooking Time: 20 minutes

4 cups chopped rhubarb

4 cups sugar

Let the rhubarb and sugar stand for 2½ hours or more, stirring occasionally.

1 small pkg. of wild strawberry
  jello

1 can crushed pineapple

Boil for 10 minutes, then add one flat can of crushed pineapple, juice and all. Let boil for 5 to 7 minutes again, take off and add one small package of undissolved wild strawberry jello. Pour into jars and seal with parafin.

Barbara VanGenderen

Tomato Soup Spice Cake or Bread

This was used during World War II when ingredients were hard to come by.

Average

Yield: One 9" x 5" loaf

Preparation Time: 15 minutes
Baking Time: 45 minutes
Oven Temperature: 375°

1 cup sugar
1 can tomato soup (1½ cups)
2 cups cake flour
4 Tbsp. shortening
1 cup nuts
1 cup raisins or dates

½ tsp. salt
1 tsp. soda
2 tsp. baking powder
1 tsp. cinnamon
1½ tsp. cloves
¼ tsp. nutmeg

Cream shortening with sugar. Stir in soup. Sift together flour, salt, spices, soda, and baking powder. Beat into shortening and soup mixture. Add nuts and raisins and pour into 9" x 5" loaf pan. Bake at 375° for 40 to 45 minutes. Serve sliced thin.

Blendine Walters

Popovers

Easy

Yield: 8

Preparation Time: 10 minutes
Baking Time: 35 minutes
Oven Temperature: 450°

2 large eggs
1 cup milk
1 cup sifted flour

½ tsp. salt
melted butter

Preheat oven to 450°. Melt butter and pour a little in each muffin cup in muffin pan. In mixing bowl, combine eggs and milk. Mix well. Add flour and salt and beat together for a few minutes. Bubbles will appear on top. Pour into muffin cups filling halfway. Bake for 15 minutes at 450° then reduce to 350° and bake 15 to 20 minutes. Do not open oven door while baking. For 16 popovers increase the eggs to three and double the rest of the ingredients.

Robin Lightner

State Fair Pretzels

These are exceptionally good and very easy.

Easy

Yield: 8 large, soft pretzels

Thawing Time: Overnight
Preparation Time: 40 minutes
Baking time: 20 minutes
Oven Temperature: 425°

1 loaf frozen bread dough

coarse salt

Let dough thaw overnight in the refrigerator or for several hours at room temperature, until it is soft enough to shape. Preheat oven to 425°. On a floured surface, cut the dough lengthwise into 8 strips. Cover and let rest for 10 minutes. Roll each strip on floured surface or between floured hands until about 18 inches long and ½ inch thick. Shape strips into pretzel shape and place on greased cookie sheet. Brush with lukewarm water. Sprinkle lightly with the coarse salt. Let rise uncovered for 15 to 20 minutes in a warm place. Place a shallow pan of water on the bottom shelf of the oven. Bake pretzels on the center shelf of the oven for 18 to 20 minutes or until brown.

Ann Danker

Zucchini Bread

Quick bread; moist and nutty! Keeps well. Batter can be prepared up to three days ahead and stored in refrigerator.

Easy

Yield: Two 1¾ lb. loaves

Preparation Time: 20 minutes
Baking Time: 1 hour
Oven Temperature: 350°

3 cups all-purpose flour
1½ cups sugar
1 cup walnuts, chopped
4½ tsp. baking powder
1 tsp. salt
4 eggs

⅔ cup salad oil
2 cups grated zucchini
2 tsp. grated lemon peel
2 tsp. vanilla
1½ tsp. cinnamon

Preheat oven to 350°. Grease two 8½ x 4½" loaf pans. In large bowl with fork, mix flour, sugar, walnuts, baking powder, and salt. In medium bowl, with fork, beat eggs slightly, stir in salad oil, zucchini and lemon peel, vanilla and cinnamon; stir into flour mixture just until flour is moistened; spread batter evenly in pans. Bake bread 1 hour or until toothpick inserted in center comes out clean. Cool in pans on wire racks 10 minutes; remove from pans. Serve bread warm or cool completely to serve cold.

Jo McKee

Banana Nut Bread

Easy

Yield: 1 large loaf or 2 small loaves

Preparation Time: 20 minutes
Baking Time:35 to 45 minutes
Oven Temperature: 325°

1 cup chopped nuts
1 cup sugar
½ cup butter
2 cups flour
2 eggs, beaten

2 Tbsp. sour milk
½ tsp. baking powder
1 tsp. soda
3 mashed bananas
pinch of salt

Cream butter and sugar. Add beaten eggs, milk with soda. Add bananas, flour, baking powder and nuts. Mix well. Pour into a large loaf pan (or two small loaf pans). Bake at 325° for 35 to 45 minutes.

Jennifer Clarke

Scandinavian Rolls

These are quick and easy and require no kneading!

Average

Yield: 24 rolls

Preparation Time: 30 minutes
Refrigerate: Overnight
Rising Time: 1 hour
Baking Time: 20 minutes
Oven Temperature: 350°

4 cups flour
¼ cup sugar
1 Tbsp. yeast
1 egg, beaten

1 tsp. salt
1 cup butter or margarine
¼ cup warm water
1 cup milk, scalded and cooled

Sift flour, salt, and sugar together. Cut in butter. Dissolve yeast in warm water; add egg and milk; blend with dry ingredients. Refrigerate overnight. Divide dough in half; roll each half into a large rectangle. Spread with soft butter and sprinkle generously with sugar and cinnamon. Roll up each rectangle and slice into 12 rolls. Let rolls rise about 1 hour. Bake at 350° until nicely browned. Remove from oven and spread with confectioner's sugar glaze flavored with almond extract. Serve warm or cold. Makes 24 rolls.

Frieda B. Chase

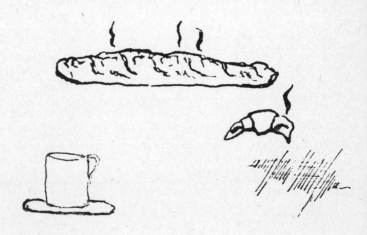

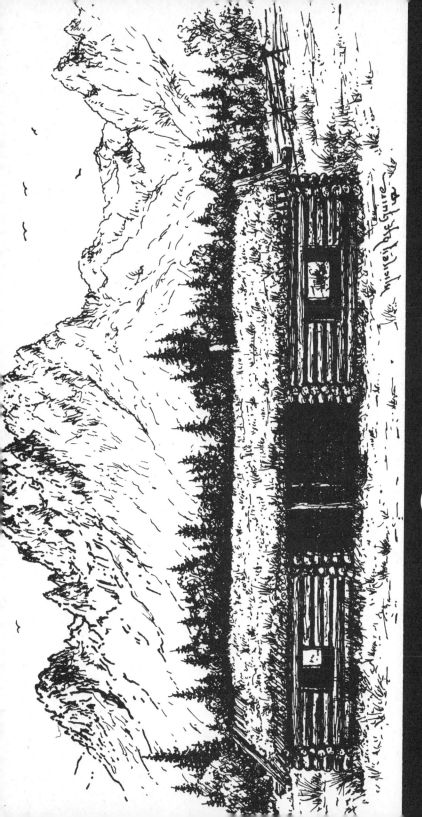

SALADS

SALADS

Cam's Lime-Pine Salad

Average
Serves: 10

Preparation Time: 30 minutes
Chilling Time: 4 hours

2 3-oz. pkgs. of lime jello
1½ cups boiling water
½ cup sour cream
½ cup mayonnaise

2 3-oz pkgs. of cream cheese
2 8-oz. cans crushed pineapple
¾ cup chopped pecans
2 Tbsp. white vinegar

Pour boiling water over jello. Stir to dissolve. In separate bowl, mix sour cream and mayonnaise to soften cream cheese. Blend. Add cream cheese mixture to gelatin and stir. This mixture should be as smooth as possible. If necessary, beat with hand or electric beater. Add remaining ingredients. Pour in a mold or pan. Refrigerate to set.

Note: For fun one year I made Christmas trees with this salad. To do this get paper cone fountain cups from drug store. Fill with gelatin salad mixture. Set in glass to hold upright. Refrigerate. Before serving, make icing. To do this, mix a little sour cream and mayonnaise to very soft cream cheese. Tint with green food coloring. Invert trees on salad plate by using a knife to help tear paper cone. Frost and decorate with bits of chopped cherries. VERY FESTIVE!!

Robin Lightner

Herbed Tomato Platter

Easy
Serves: 6

Preparation Time: 15 minutes
Chilling Time: 3 hours or more

6 ripe tomatoes
⅔ cup salad oil
¼ cup vinegar
¼ cup chopped parsley

¼ cup sliced green onions
1 tsp. salt
½ tsp. coarsely ground pepper

Peel tomatoes. Place in deep bowl. Combine oil, vinegar, and seasonings. Shake well. Pour over tomatoes. Chill at least several hours or overnight. Occasionally spoon dressing over the tomatoes. At serving time transfer the tomatoes to serving platter. Spoon dressing over. Cucumber slices are a good addition to this mixture if the tomatoes are sliced rather than whole.

Martha Clark

Jellied Beet Salad

This is good served with meats, especially game.

Easy
Serves: 6

Preparation Time: 15 minutes
Chilling Time: 3 hours

1 3-oz. pkg. lemon Jell-o
1 cup celery
½ cup walnuts, chopped

1 16-oz. can diced beets
2 tsp. horseradish

Drain liquid from beet can and reserve to mix with the gelatin. Mix Jell-o according to directions using beet juice and enough water to make the cup of cold water. Add the other ingredients and pour into mold. Amount of horseradish may vary according to taste. (Two teaspoons make a snappy salad. Some people might prefer only one teaspoon.)

Jo Case

Cranberry Salad "Vetah"

This is our traditional family salad for Thanksgiving and Christmas.

Easy   *Preparation Time: 40 minutes*
Serves: 10   *Chilling Time: 2 to 3 hours*

2 pkgs. raspberry jello
2 cups hot water
1 small can crushed pineapple
1 can whole cranberry sauce

1 cup broken pecans
¾ cups port wine
1 pint sour cream
1 3-oz. pkg. cream cheese

Mix raspberry jello in hot water until dissolved. Add cranberry sauce, pineapple, pecans, and port. Put in refrigerator until set. Meanwhile, beat sour cream and cream cheese together until smooth. When salad is set, spread sour cream mixture over it. Use a large (13 x 9 x 2") pan for salad. You can make this a day ahead and cover with Saran Wrap and refrigerate until ready to serve.

Marge D'Atri

Frozen Cranberry Salad

An excellent salad to serve with chicken or turkey.

Easy   *Preparation Time: 20 minutes*
Yield: Serves 6   *Freezing Time: 3 hours*

2 3-oz. size pkg. of cream cheese
2 Tbsp. sugar
1 small can crushed pineapple,
   drained

1 cup heavy cream, whipped
2 Tbsp. mayonnaise
1 can whole cranberry sauce
½ cup chopped nuts

Cream together the cream cheese, mayonnaise and sugar. Add cranberry sauce, pineapple and nuts. Fold in the whipped cream and put in a 9" square pan. Freeze for about 3 hours. Take out of freezer a few minutes before serving, but serve fairly frozen.

Jo Case

Frozen Banana Salad

This salad is especially nice when you are busy.

Easy
Yield: Serves 6

Preparation Time: 15 minutes
Freezing Time: 3 hours

2 bananas, mashed
¾ cup sugar
½ cup pecans, chopped
2 cups sour cream

1 small can crushed pineapple,
  drained
2 Tbsp. chopped cherries
2 Tbsp. lemon juice

Blend all ingredients except sour cream thoroughly, then add sour cream. Mix well and pour into 9" square pan and freeze for three hours. Remove from freezer and cut into squares to serve.

Helpful Hint: You can fill muffin tins lined with cupcake papers and freeze, then put the individual servings in a plastic bag in the freezer and they will keep until the time comes when you need a little 'something special.'

Robin Lightner

Raspberry Salad

Good with poultry

Easy
Serves: 12

Preparation Time: 15 minutes
Refrigeration Time: 4 hours or more

2 cups boiling water
2 pkgs. of raspberry jello
2 cups applesauce

2 pkgs. of partially thawed frozen
  red raspberries

Dissolve jello in 2 cups of boiling water. Add the raspberries and applesauce. Pour into a mold and refrigerate until set.

Marta Winger

Marinated Carrots

Serve in crockery for casual or pretty glass dish for company.

Average　　　　　　　　　　*Preparation Time: 30 minutes*
Yield: 2 quarts　　　　　　　　　*Chilling Time: 12 hours*

5 cups of sliced cooked
　carrots (2 bunches)
1 medium onion, sliced thin
1 green pepper, sliced
1 can of tomato soup, undiluted
½ cup vegetable oil

1 cup sugar
1 tsp. prepared mustard
¾ cup vinegar
1 tsp. Worcestershire sauce
1 tsp. salt
1 tsp. pepper

Drain and cool carrots; add onion and pepper. Mix gently. In a saucepan, combine remaining ingredients and bring to boil over medium heat. Cool and pour over carrots, onion, and pepper. Cover and refrigerate for at least 12 hours. Keeps well.

Jane Skeoch

Orange Cloud Salad

Easy　　　　　　　　　　　*Preparation Time: 10 minutes*
Serves: 8　　　　　　　　　*Refrigeration Time: 2 hours*

1 large carton Cool Whip
1 16-oz. carton cottage cheese,
　small curd
1 large box orange Jello

1 small can crushed pineapple,
　drained
2 cans mandarin oranges, drained

Mix dry Jello and cottage cheese well. Then add the remaining ingredients, reserving one can of mandarin oranges to decorate the top of the salad. Refrigerate for about two hours and serve.

This can be cut down to small containers of cottage cheese, jello and cool whip for a smaller salad. You may also use different flavors of jello and fruits.

Ada Clark

Tomato Aspic

Average
Serves: 4

Preparation Time: 20 minutes
Chilling Time: 2 hours

1 pkg. unflavored gelatin
2 cups V-8 Juice
1 tsp. Lawrys seasoned salt
1 Tbsp. Worcestershire Sauce
5 drops Tabasco Sauce
2 tsp. lemon juice

2 Tbsp. dried parsley
½ cups chopped celery
½ cup green onions
½ cup cooked, small shrimp
mayonnaise

Soften gelatin in ½ cup V-8 Juice. Add salt, Worcestershire Sauce, Tabasco, and lemon juice to rest of V-8 Juice. Add gelatin mixture and heat to boiling, stirring constantly. Cook until gelatin is completely dissolved. Allow it to cool. Add parsley flakes, celery, green onions, and shrimp. Pour into mold and refrigerate until set. Serve with a dollop of mayonnaise.

Marge D'Atri

Swiss Egg Salad

Easy

Preparation Time: 30 minutes

½ lb. Swiss cheese, cut in
   1 inch strips
½ cup sour cream
1 tsp. grated horseradish
½ tsp. salt
crisp salad greens

6 hard cooked eggs, finely
   chopped
1½ tsp. dry mustard
pinch of ground cumin seed
½ tsp. pepper

Toss all the ingredients together. Arrange the salad on a bed of crisp salad greens.

Alice Glass

Wilted Spinach Salad

I have tried many spinach salads, and most were too sour. This one is great!!

Average
Serves: 4

Preparation Time: 30 minutes

1 lb. spinach—washed, dried, and
   torn in bite-size pieces
6 green onions, chopped
1 Tbsp. salad oil
3 slices bacon, fried until crisp
   and crumbled

1 clove garlic
1 egg
1 Tbsp. sugar
1 Tbsp. tarragon vinegar
1 Tbsp. red wine vinegar
salt and pepper

Put torn spinach in bowl. Let garlic clove stand in salad oil. Chop green onions. Fry bacon and remove from pan. Reserve bacon fat in skillet. Beat together egg, sugar, vinegars. Add a little salt and pepper. Meanwhile, pour oil over spinach. Just before ready to serve, pour egg mixture into warm bacon grease stirring constantly. Immediately pour over spinach. Sprinkle with bacon and serve.

Robin Lightner

Taco Salad

This would be a good one-dish meal served with hot bread.

Easy
Yield: Serves 10

Preparation Time: 20 minutes

1 15½-oz. can red kidney beans,
   drained
1 7-oz. bag taco flavored
   corn chips
4 large tomatoes, diced

1 cup grated cheese
1 lb. hamburger
1 head lettuce
1 onion, chopped
1 pkg. taco seasoning mix

Cook hamburger until crumbly and brown. Put torn lettuce in salad bowl and follow with other ingredients. You may refrigerate at this time. Just before serving, add Italian dressing or oil and vinegar dressing and toss.

Roberta Richardson

Marinated Bean Salad

Excellent accompaniment to outdoor cooking.

Easy
Yield: Serves 16

Preparation Time: 25 minutes
Chilling Time: Overnight

1 can green beans, drained
1 can red kidney beans,
  rinsed and drained
1 can blackeyed peas, rinsed
  and drained

1 can yellow wax beans, drained
1 can lima beans, drained
1 medium green pepper, sliced
  in rings
1 medium onion, sliced in rings

MARINADE:

½ cup sugar
½ cup salad oil
½ tsp. dry mustard
½ tsp. basil

½ cup wine vinegar
1 tsp. salt
½ tsp. dried tarragon leaves
2 Tbsp. parsley

Place all the ingredients in bowl, cover and marinate over-night in the refrigerator. Stir once or twice. Drain just prior to serving.

Robin Lightner

Sauerkraut Salad

Great for potlucks!! The longer it stands, the better it tastes!!

Easy
Serves: 6

Preparation Time: 30 minutes
Refrigeration Time: Overnight

1 1-lb. can of raw sauerkraut
  with juice
½ cup finely diced celery
½ cup finely diced onion
½ cup finely diced green pepper
2½ Tbsp. sugar

2 Tbsp. vinegar
salt and pepper to taste
4 to 5 oz. of Wishbone Italian
  Salad Dressing
2 Tbsp. chopped pimentos,
  optional

Mix all ingredients together. Place in jar—refrigerate over-night—inverting the jar every so often. The salad will stay fresh for over a week.

Nancy L. Wiegand Schweinfurth

Spinach Salad Supreme

This is very easy and very good.

Easy   *Preparation Time: 20 minutes*
Yield: Serves 6

4 slices of fried bacon, drained   3 Tbsp. wine vinegar
4 Tbsp. fine grade olive oil   2 hard cooked eggs, peeled
1 lb. raw spinach, washed   and diced
   and drained   freshly ground black pepper
1 small white onion, thinly sliced   salt
1 Tbsp. bacon drippings

Crumble fried bacon, drain on paper towel. In a small bowl or glass jar, combine bacon drippings, olive oil and vinegar. Mix well and set aside. Place spinach, eggs, onion, and bacon crumbles in salad bowl. Season well with salt and pepper. Sprinkle with dressing and toss.

Jeanne Houfek

Spinach Swinger Salad

This is a super different molded salad.

Easy   *Preparation Time: 20 minutes*
Yield: 1½ quart mold   *Chill Time: 2 hours*

2 envelopes unflavored gelatine   ¼ cup water
1 10-oz. can condensed beef broth   ½ tsp. salt
   (or 2 cubes in 1 cup water)   1 cup mayonnaise
2 Tbsp. lemon juice   4 hard cooked eggs
1 10-oz. pkg. frozen chopped   ¼ cup chopped onion
   spinach, thawed   pimento strips
½ lb. cooked bacon, crumbled

Soften gelatine in broth, stir over low heat until dissolved. Stir in water, salt and lemon juice. Gradually add gelatine to mayonnaise, mixing until well blended. Chill until slightly thickened. Fold in well drained spinach, onions, eggs and bacon. Pour into 1½ quart mold. Chill until firm. Garnish with pimento. *Hint:* Hard salami cut up can be used instead of bacon.

Jo Case

Spinach Salad

An unusual and delicious spinach salad.

Easy   *Preparation Time: 15 minutes*
Yield: Serves 5 to 6

1 bag of spinach
½ cup chopped onion
   (red, white, or green)
2 hard cooked eggs, sliced

3 slices cooked bacon, crumbled
horseradish
¾ cups grated sharp Cheddar
   cheese

DRESSING:
½ cup mayonnaise
   (not salad dressing or Miracle
   Whip)

1 tsp. lemon juice
salt and pepper to taste
½ cup sour cream

Mix dressing ingredients together and thin with milk or cream if necessary. Place all the salad ingredients except horseradish in a bowl and toss with the dressing. Serve with dollops of horseradish on the side.

Ellie Wiegand

Honey Fruit Dressing

Easy   *Preparation Time: 5 minutes*
Yield: 1 ½ cups   *Cooking Time: 10 minutes*

1 cup honey
⅓ cup lime juice

⅓ cup creme sherry
2 sticks cinnamon

Combine all ingredients in saucepan and heat slowly. Simmer for ten minutes, covered. Pour into glass jar and refrigerate. Will keep for months.

Lee Jensen

Tomato-Cream Cheese Salad

Good with any entree'!

Easy
Serves: 12

Preparation Time: 15 minutes
Refrigeration Time: 2 to 3 hours

1 can tomato soup
3 small pkgs. cream cheese
2 Tbsp. plain gelatin, dissolved
   in ½ cup cold water
1 cup mayonnaise
1½ cups chopped celery

1 small bottle stuffed olives,
   chopped
green pepper and onion in small
   quantity. Top with more mayonnaise

Bring soup to boil, add cheese, stir until smooth: add gelatin softened in cold water. When cool, add salad dressing and vegetables and put into individual molds. Refrigerate until firm. To serve, unmold and top with more mayonnaise.

Martha Winger

Low Calorie Blue Cheese Dressing

Easy
Yield: 1 ½ cups

Preparation Time: 5 minutes

1 cup plain yogurt
8 Tbsp. blue cheese, crumbled
2 tsp. sugar

½ tsp. celery seed
dash of Tabasco

In a blender, put two tablespoons of blue cheese with the rest of the ingredients. Turn on the blender until mixed. Fold in remaining cheese. If too thick, this can be thinned with butter-milk.

Lee Jensen

G. BLANDICK

ENTREES

MEATS

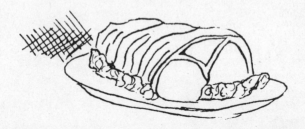

Apricot Glazed Brisket

Average
Serves: 6 to 8

Cooking Time: 3 hours
Broiling Time: 20 to 30 minutes

1 boneless beef brisket (3½ lbs.)
  or a wild game brisket
1 medium onion stuck with
  2 cloves
1 clove garlic, halved
1 bay leaf
2 Tbsp. plus 2 tsp. salt

2 jars (7¾ oz. size) junior apricots
¼ cup vegetable oil
2 Tbsp. cider vinegar
1 Tbsp. ketchup
4 tsp. sugar
1 tsp. ground allspice
water

Place brisket, onion stuck with cloves, garlic, bay leaf, two tablespoons salt and enough water to cover in 6 quart Dutch oven or a saucepan. Heat to boiling. Reduce heat to low; cover and simmer 2½ to 3 hours, or until brisket is fork-tender. Remove brisket; cover and refrigerate (discard broth). Stir together apricots, vegetable oil, vinegar, ketchup, sugar and allspice and two teaspoons salt. Place brisket on rack in broiler pan. Broil 20 to 30 minutes, six inches from heating element, until hot, turning occasionally. During last ten minutes, baste brisket frequently with apricot mixture. (If cooking and serving the same day, broil only 8 to 10 minutes, brushing with apricot glaze.) Heat remaining mixture to serve with meat.

Jo Case

60

Barbequed Pot Roast

Dress up your pot roast and make it company fare.

Easy
Serves: 6 to 8

Preparation Time: 15 minutes
Cooking Time: 2 to 3 hours

3 lbs. beef pot roast
2 tsp. salt
¼ tsp. pepper
3 Tbsp. salad oil
½ cup water
1 small can tomato sauce
3 medium onions, chopped
2 cloves garlic

2 Tbsp. brown sugar
¼ tsp. paprika
½ tsp. dry mustard
¼ cup lemon juice
¼ cup catsup
¼ cup vinegar
1 Tbsp. Worcestershire sauce

Brown meat in oil. Add water, tomato sauce, onion and minced garlic. Simmer for 1½ hours. Combine remaining ingredients and pour over meat. Cook about one hour longer or until tender. Thicken gravy with paste made of flour and water.

Marge D'Atri

Beef Jerky

Easy

Yield: about 2 lbs.

Preparation Time: 20 minutes
Marinate Time: 6 to 8 hours
Oven Temperature: 200°

¼ cup soy sauce
2 tsp. garlic salt
3 lbs. lean meat such as round
   steak or game

¾ cups of water
¼ tsp. black pepper

Select thick, lean meat such as round steak and freeze. Later, partially thaw and trim off all fat. Slice thinly into 1/8 inch strips. Cover meat with marinade solution for 2 to 3 hours then drain on paper towels and pat dry. Lay the strips of meat across an oven rack, avoiding any overlapping. In low oven, dry for 6 to 8 hours until meat becomes brittle. Only well-trimmed meat will work properly since any fat that remains will become rancid. Store in an air-tight container.

Jo Case

A Favorite Casserole

Use any ground beef or game meat.

Average

Serves: 6 to 8

Preparation Time: 30 minutes
Baking Time: 1 hour
Oven Temperature: 375°

2 cups uncooked noodles
2 medium onions, sliced
1 Tbsp. butter or margarine
1 lb. ground beef or game meat
1 cup cottage cheese

1 cup milk
1 can cream of mushroom soup
1½ tsp. salt
½ cup grated Cheddar cheese
2 eggs, beaten

Cook noodles in boiling water until barely tender; drain and rinse. In large skillet, saute sliced onion in butter until light yellow; set aside. In same skillet, cook ground meat, stirring to break into bits. Add sauteed onion and cottage cheese. In 2 quart casserole, arrange one third of noodles, then half meat mixture. Repeat. Place remaining noodles on top. Combine milk, mushroom soup and salt; pour over casserole. Sprinkle grated cheese over top; pour beaten eggs over cheese. Bake uncovered in moderate oven, 375°, for 1 hour.

Fran Mosley

Marinated Flank Steak

Easy

Serves: 2 to 4

Preparation Time: 10 minutes
Marinate Time: All day
Cooking Time: 14 minutes

1 flank steak
2 Tbsp. white sugar
½ tsp. ground ginger
¼ cup hot water
½ cup Kikkoman soy sauce

¼ cup Lea and Perrins Worcestershire sauce
¼ tsp. garlic powder
¼ tsp. thyme
¼ tsp. sage

In shallow bowl dissolve 2 Tbsp. sugar and ½ tsp. ginger in ¼ cup hot water. Add other ingredients. Make up marinade the night before use. Add steak in the morning. If it is not covered by marinade, turn over around noon. When ready to cook, remove steak from marinade and brown in hot skillet about 7 minutes on each side. Slice steak into thin diagonal slices and serve.

Greg McHuron

Flank Steak Roulades

Average   *Preparation Time: 30 minutes*
Serves: 6   *Cooking Time: 1½ hours*

FILLING:

1 can crabmeat, drained   1 large flank steak
½ cup Parmesan cheese   1 cup bouillion
½ cup soft bread crumbs   Worcestershire sauce
6 Tbsp. artichoke hearts,   salt and pepper
   drained, chopped, marinated
1 cup sour cream

Combine filling ingredients and set aside. Cut flank steak into six lengths, each one an inch wide. Beat steak flat until it's about two inches wide. Sprinkle with salt and pepper and Worcestershire sauce. Divide filling equally onto the six steaks. Roll into two inch wide rolls and tie securely with string. Brown in butter. Add 1 cup bouillion to steak. Cover and simmer for 1½ hours.

Irene Brown

Zippy Chuck Roast

This is good enough for company. It is also super with short ribs instead of chuck roast.

Easy   *Preparation Time: 15 minutes*
Serves: 4 to 6   *Cooking Time: 2½ to 3 hours*

1 boneless chuck roast, 1½ inches   1 Tbsp. soy sauce
   thick, 2 to 3 pounds   2 Tbsp. brown sugar
1 Tbsp. salad oil   ¼ tsp. garlic powder
1 7-oz. can Ortega Chili Salsa   1 tsp. salt

Brown meat well in large skillet or Dutch oven. Mix remaining ingredients together and pour over browned meat. Cover tightly and simmer for 2½ to 3 hours or until meat is tender. Add water during cooking, if necessary. Skim fat and serve steak with remaining sauce. If you prefer, bake steak in a plastic cooking bag following bag directions for pot roast.

Marge D'Atri

Carbonnade A La Flammande

Average   *Preparation Time: 30 minutes*
Serves: 4 to 6   *Cooking Time: 2 hours*

2½ lbs. beef rump or chuck roast   3 Tbsp. lard
  (elk or deer could be used)   ¼ cup brown sugar
2 to 3 large onions   1 garlic clove
2 Tbsp. vinegar   1 bay leaf
pinch of thyme   slice of crusty bread
1 can of beer   Dijon-style mustard

Cut meat into 10 to 14 slices and flatten with cleaver. Brown meat in lard or fat and put in heavy casserole. In fat remaining in pan, lightly brown onions, thinly sliced. Sprinkle with brown sugar and shake pan over medium heat until carmelized. Sprinkle onions with vinegar and add the contents of skillet to casserole. Add 1 garlic clove, finely chopped, a pinch of thyme, one bay leaf, and enough beer to cover meat completely. Spread a large slice of crusty bread thickly with Dijon-style mustard and put on top of meat. Bring just to a boil, cover casserole, and simmer over lowest possible heat for about two hours or until beer is reduced by half. If beer is not reducing fast enough, remove lid for last 15 minutes of cooking. The bread will completely dissolve, binding the sauce. Serve with steamed potatoes, scallions, and cold beer.

Jo Case

Texas' Herman Sons Stuff Burgers

Easy   *Preparation Time: 15 minutes*
Yield: 4   *Cooking Time: 15 minutes*

2 lbs. hamburger meat   2 cups grated Cheddar cheese
1 onion, chopped   Optional: chopped green chilies

Mix onion, cheese and green chilies. Make eight large patties. Top four patties with a generous amount of cheese mixture. Top with another pattie. Seal edges together. Broil, fry or charcoal. Season with salt and pepper.

Robin Lightner

More
(Ground Meat and Vegetable Dish)

Good potluck dish.

Easy   *Preparation Time: 30 minutes*
                                              Cooking Time: 1 hour
Serves: 10   *Oven Temperature: 350°*

1 lb. hamburger   1 can mushrooms
½ lb. ground pork   1 can pitted, ripe olives
1 onion, chopped   1½ cups uncooked rice
1 No. 2 can peas   ½ lb. grated cheese
1 No. 2½ can tomatoes   1 can pimentoes, chopped

Fry hamburger, pork, onion until almost done. Add other ingredients, put in large baking dish and cover. Bake one hour at 350⁰. Add tomato juice for more liquid if needed.

Louise Murie-MacLeod

Picadillo

Excellent!!—Can be done ahead of time.

Average   *Preparation Time: 20 minutes*
Serves: 6   *Baking Time: 30 minutes*

1 lb. ground meat   2 Tbsp. dark brown sugar
1 onion, chopped   1 tsp. capers
1 green pepper, chopped   ⅓ cup raisins
1 clove garlic, sliced   1 small bottle stuffed olives
1 8-oz. can tomato sauce

In 2 Tbsp. vegetable oil, fry onion, green pepper, and garlic, slowly. When tender, remove from skillet and brown meat in same fat. Add the onions, pepper, and garlic to meat. Add tomato sauce, capers, sugar, and raisins. Allow to simmer slowly. Just before serving, add stuffed olives. Serve on rice, OR, this dish can be served as a dip with tortilla chips.

Louise Murie-Macleod

Stir-Fried Beef with Vegetables

Average   *Preparation Time: 20 minutes*
Serves: 4   *Cooking Time: 15 minutes*

1 lb. boneless round steak   1 medium onion
1 Tbsp. sugar   4 Tbsp. vegetable oil
1 Tbsp. cornstarch   1 can water chestnuts or
2 Tbsp. dry sherry   bamboo shoots
3 Tbsp. soy sauce   1 tsp. salt
1 lb. fresh green beans

Cut beef across grain into 1/8" thick slices. Place beef in a
bowl. Add sugar, cornstarch, sherry, and soy sauce. Toss until
mixed. Cut beans into 2" diagonal pieces; slice onion; put
vegetables into large bowl. Heat large deep skillet or wok over
high heat. Add 2 Tbsp. of the oil; swirl to coat bottom and sides
of pan. Add beans and onion. Stir fry until pieces are coated
with oil. Add water chestnuts; toss; cover. Cook until beans are
tender-crisp. Remove vegetables to large bowl. Discard cooking liquid. Reheat pan. Add remaining oil, swirl to coat bottom,
add half of marinated beef. Stir fry just until browned. Remove
to bowl of vegetables. Stir fry remaining beef. Return vegetables and beef to pan. Add salt; toss to mix. Spoon onto warm
plates, serve with rice.

Sandy Bommer

Chili

A delicious dish to serve on cold nights.

Easy   *Preparation Time: 30 minutes*
Serves: 8   *Cooking Time: 5 hours*

1½ lbs. ground beef or elk
½ lb. pork sausage
2 medium chopped onions
2 garlic cloves
¼ bell pepper, chopped
1 can tomatoes/green chilies
1 28-oz. can peeled tomatoes
2 cans kidney or pinto beans,
    drained

1 small can tomato sauce
2 Tbsp. chili powder
1 Tbsp. Worcestershire sauce
¼ tsp. thyme
¼ tsp. ground cumin
¼ tsp. oregano
salt and pepper to taste
28 oz. water
2 Tbsp. bacon grease

Brown the ground meat and sausage in 2 Tbsp. bacon grease. Add the chopped onions, garlic, and bell pepper. Continue cooking for a few minutes. Add the rest of the ingredients (except for the beans), adding the water last. Use the empty tomato can to measure the water. There should be enough water, but you may need to add more during the cooking. Simmer the chili covered for five hours or longer if you wish. Add the beans (if desired) the last 30 minutes of cooking. Serve with small bowls of chopped onion and grated cheese. This makes a complete meal with cornbread and salad.

Robin Lightner

Stroganoff Beefburgers

Easy
Serves: 8

Preparation Time: 30 minutes

1 lb. ground beef
3 slices bacon, diced
½ cup chopped onion
1 can condensed cream of
   mushroom soup

1½ Tbsp. flour
1 cup yogurt
½ tsp. salt
8 hamburger buns, split and
   toasted

Brown ground beef and bacon. Add onion, cook until tender. Drain off excess fat. Blend flour and seasonings into meat mixture. Stir in soup. Cook slowly uncovered for 20 minutes stirring frequently. Stir in yogurt and heat through but do not boil. Serve on toasted buns.

Clare Joy

Barbecued Ribs

Average

Serves: 10 to 12

Preparation Time: 20 minutes
Baking Time: 1 ½ hours
Oven Temperature: 350°

3 lbs pork spareribs
1 to 2 Tbsp. liquid smoke
1 cup catsup
¼ cup Worcestershire sauce
¼ cup lemon juice
1 tsp. salt
1 tsp. chili powder
1 cup water

1 tsp. celery seed
1 onion, grated
2 to 3 squirts Tabasco sauce
1/8 tsp. prepared mustard
1/8 tsp. paprika
1/8 tsp. black pepper
1/8 tsp. cayene pepper
2 to 3 Tbsp. brown sugar

Put liquid smoke on ribs and cook in 350⁰ oven for 30 minutes. Prepare and cook sauce. Put sauce on ribs and return to oven for 1 to 1½ hours at 350⁰.

Jennifer Clark

Swedish Meat Balls

Easy
Yield: 2 dozen

Preparation Time: 15 minutes
Cooking Time: 20 minutes

¼ cup chopped onion
1 Tbsp. butter or margarine
½ lb. ground beef
½ lb. ground veal
¾ tsp. salt

dash of white pepper
2 Tbsp. enriched flour
1 egg
¼ cup light cream
1 can consomme

Cook onions in butter until tender but not brown. Combine meat and seasonings. Beat thoroughly. Beat in flour. Add eggs. Gradually beat in cream. Beat in onions. This mixture should be light and fluffy. Form mixture into one inch balls and lightly brown in additional butter. Shake skillet to turn balls. Remove excess fat. Add consomme and cook uncovered 12 to 15 minutes. If desired, thicken gravy with flour or cornstarch.

Anna Scrivens

Pork Chops King

Easy

Serves: 4

Preparation Time: 15 minutes
Baking Time: 1 hour
Oven Temperature: 300°

4 pork chops, or sliced pork
 tenderloins
½ lemon, sliced thin
½ onion, sliced thin

½ green pepper, sliced thin
½ tomato, sliced thin
½ sour cream
¼ cup chili sauce

Brown pork on both sides and place in a shallow pan or casserole dish. Cover each piece with thin slices of lemon, onion, tomato and green pepper with lemon next to the meat. Mix chili sauce with sour cream until it is a pretty pink. Spoon over the meat and vegetables. Bake at 300⁰ for an hour or more.

Kay King

Yummy Pork Chops

Easy   *Preparation Time: 20 minutes*
                                                      Baking Time: 1 hour
Serves: 6   *Oven Temperature: 350°*

6 pork chops   ¾ cup water
2 Tbsp. flour   ½ tsp. ginger
1 tsp. salt   ¼ tsp. rosemary
pepper   1 can onion rings
1 can cream of mushroom soup   1 cup sour cream

Salt and pepper chops dredged in flour. Brown in hot fat.
Place in baking dish. Combine soup, water, ginger, and rosemary. Pour over chops and sprinkle half of onion rings on top.
Cover. Bake for 50 minutes. Uncover, sprinkle remaining onion
rings over top, bake 10 minutes. Remove to platter. Blend sour
cream in sauce and serve with fluffy rice.

Robin Lightner

Ham Loaf

Average   *Preparation Time: 15 minutes*
                                                      Baking Time: 1½ hours
Yield: Two 9 x 5 x 3" loaf pans   *Oven Temperature: 350°*

2 lbs. ground ham   1 cup milk
1½ lbs. lean ground pork   1 cup dry bread crumbs
2 eggs
GLAZE:
¾ cup brown sugar   ¼ cup vinegar
¼ cup water   2 tsp. dry mustard

Combine glaze ingredients and set aside. Combine ham
loaf ingredients and pack in loaf pans or form into loaves and
place on baking sheets. Bake in a 350° oven for 1½ hours,
basting frequently with glaze.

Irene Brown

Pork Chops with Green Chili Salsa

This is sure to make a hit with everyone.

Easy   Preparation Time: 15 minutes
                                        Baking Time: 30 to 40 minutes
Serves: 4   Oven Temperature: 325°

4 large pork chops   1 can Ortega green chili salsa
1 Tbsp. salad oil   1 cup water
1 cup uncooked rice   1 tsp. salt
paprika

Preheat oven to 325°. Sprinkle chops with paprika. Brown chops well in salad oil. Remove from pan. Saute rice in pan for 2 to 3 minutes. Add chili salsa, water, and salt. Put rice in a greased casserole. Place chops on top. Cover and bake at 325° for 30 to 40 minutes or until rice is tender.

Marge D'Atri

Barbequed Leg of Lamb

Short ribs of beef are also fabulous when braised with this sauce.

Easy   Preparation Time: 10 minutes
                                        Baking Time: 2½ hours
Serves: 6   Oven Temperature: 325°

5 lb. leg of lamb   2 Tbsp. Lea and Perrins
2 tsp. salt   ½ tsp. thyme
½ tsp. pepper   1 medium onion, chopped
1 can beef broth   ¼ tsp. garlic powder
3 Tbsp. vinegar

Sprinkle lamb with salt and pepper. Place in shallow roasting pan in preheated 325° oven. Mix broth, catsup, vinegar, Lea and Perrins, thyme, onion, and garlic powder. Bring to a boil and pour over lamb. Roast lamb 2 to 2½ hours or until done to your liking. Baste frequently with the sauce. Add more water to sauce as it is needed. When lamb is done, remove from pan and keep warm. Skim fat from sauce and add some water, if it is too strong. Serve sauce with the sliced lamb.

Marge D'Atri

Leg of Lamb with Plum Sauce

Easy

Serves: 5 to 6

Preparation Time: 15 minutes
Cooking Time: 2½ to 3 hours
Oven Temperature: 325°

1 leg of lamb
salt and pepper
2 10-oz. jars of plum jelly
¼ cup lemon juice

2 Tbsp. soy sauce
2 tsp. Worcestershire sauce
1 tsp. basil, crushed
1 clove garlic, crushed

Season lamb with salt and pepper. Place fat side up on a rack in a roasting pan. Roast in 325° oven for 2½ to 3 hours or until meat thermometer reads 175°. Mix remaining ingredients and baste lamb several times during last hour of cooking. Simmer remaining sauce and serve with meat.

Robin Lightner

Beef Stroganoff

A quick and easy version of a fancy dish.

Easy
Serves: 4

Preparation Time: 25 minutes

1½ lbs. of steak cut in strips
1 chopped onion
1 large can mushrooms
1 can beef gravy

1 pint sour cream
2 Tbsp. salad oil
1 8-oz. pkg. noodles

Saute onion and mushrooms in salad oil until onion is tender. Remove from pan. Quickly saute steak strips until medium rare. Return onion and mushrooms to pan and add beef gravy and sour cream. Remove from heat. Cook noodles according to package directions. When noodles are done, reheat beef stroganoff but do not boil or sour cream will curdle. Serve over noodles.

Marge D'Atri

POULTRY

Popover Chicken

This is a delicious and unusual way to serve chicken.

Average

Serves: 4

Preparation Time: 30 minutes
Baking Time: 50 to 60 minutes
Oven Temperature: 350°

2½ to 3 lbs. broiler-fryer, cut up
3 eggs
1½ cups milk
1½ cups sifted flour

¾ tsp. salt
1 Tbsp. cooking oil
1 Tbsp. fresh Tarragon -OR-
   1 tsp. dried Tarragon

MUSHROOM SAUCE:
1 3-oz. can mushrooms, drained
1 Tbsp. butter
¼ cup milk

1 can condensed cream of mush-
   soup

    Brown chicken in 2 Tbsp. cooking oil. Season with a little salt and pepper. Place chicken in one layer in a well greased, shallow 2 quart baking dish. In mixing bowl combine eggs, milk, flour and salt. Beat 1½ minutes with rotary or electric beater. Add oil and tarragon. Beat 30 seconds more. Do not overbeat. Pour over chicken. Bake in moderate oven (350º) for 50 to 60 minutes or until done and golden brown. Serve with the following sauce.

MUSHROOM SAUCE: In a sauce pan cook mushrooms in butter for 4 to 5 minutes. Add soup and gradually stir in the ¼ cup of milk. Heat through.

Jo Case

Chicken Farrier

I named this dish after watching a friend prepare it about 18 years ago—he was a horseshoer.

Average   *Preparation Time: 1 hour*
Serves: 4 to 6

small fyer pieces (we like breasts so I cut them in half)
one loaf of high round sourdough French bread
½ lb. of butter, altogether
2 Tbsp. olive oil
2 to 3 large cloves of garlic
1 tsp. rosemary
salt to taste
pepper to taste

½ to ¾ lb. of fresh mushrooms
fresh parsley
¾ cup of dry sherry
one can of green ripe olives

Saute small fryer pieces in butter and a little olive oil and garlic. Add rosemary, salt and pepper to taste. While that is cooking, cut top out of French loaf; remove insides and reserve for bread crumbs or bread pudding. Put into oven to toast lightly. Rub with garlic inside and out when toasted, and butter.

Saute mushrooms separately in butter.

When chicken is almost done, add parsley and dry sherry. Simmer. Add green ripe olives and mushrooms. Fit chicken pieces into bread; pour juice over; dip top into saute pan to remove last of juices. Put finished bread filled into oven for five minutes at 350°.

Serve on a platter and have everyone "dig in" taking a piece of chicken and tearing off a piece of bread.

I always serve terry cloth napkins with this dish!!!

Wynne Gensey

Chicken Enchiladas

These are excellent and freeze beautifully.

Average

Serves: 12 to 15

Preparation Time: 45 minutes
Baking Time: 30 minutes
Oven Temperature: 325° to 350°

1 3 to 4 lb. hen
1½ cups onion, chopped
1 28-oz. can tomatoes
1 2-lb box Velveeta cheese
30 corn tortillas
2 cups sour cream
cooking oil

½ cup butter
2 10-oz. can tomatoes & green
    chilies (Rotel brand if possible)
    -OR- 1 28-oz. can tomatoes and
    1 4-oz. can diced Ortega green
    chilies

Boil and bone chicken. Cool and tear into bite-size pieces. Saute onions slowly in butter until tender. Drain tomatoes reserving liquid. Add tomatoes, breaking them up, to onion and simmer until thick. Cut up cheese and add, stirring until melted. Add chicken. Mixture should be thick. If too thick, add juice from canned tomatoes.

Fry tortillas in oil over medium heat to soften—about 30 seconds. Drain on paper towels. Place heaping tablespoon of chicken mixture in each tortilla and roll up. Place in baking dish. Pour remaining chicken mixture on top of enchiladas. Spread sour cream over top and bake at 350° in glass pan or 325° in metal pan about 30 minutes.

If you wish, you may freeze before adding the sour cream. When ready to serve, remove from freezer one hour before baking. Spread with sour cream. Bake 40-45 minutes.

Robin Lightner

Contemporary Chicken Bake

This is an excellent, quick and easy luncheon dish.

Average

Serves: 10 to 12

Preparation Time: 45 minutes
Cooking Time: 45 minutes
Oven Temperature: 350°

2 chicken bouillon cubes
1 cup boiling water
1 egg, slightly beaten
7 to 8-oz. pkg. Herb Season
  Stuffing Mix
1 cup Pet evaporated milk
2½ cups cut-up chicken or
  turkey, cooked

1 can cream of mushroom soup
⅔ cup Pet evaporated milk
2 Tbsp. finely cut pimento
½ cup shredded process
  American cheese

Dissolve the bouillon cubes in the boiling water and let cool. Mix in a large bowl, the egg, the seasoned stuffing mix and one cup of evaporated milk and bouillon. Spread this mixture in a shallow, well-greased two quart baking dish. Sprinkle the chopped chicken or turkey over this then pour the mushroom soup, mixed with the ⅔ cup of Pet evaporated milk and the chopped pimento over the chopped chicken, then sprinkle top with shredded Process American Cheese. Cover with aluminum foil and bake for 45 minutes at 350°. Uncover and bake 10 minutes more.

Freida Chase

Chicken A La Francaise

Easy

Serves: 6

Preparation Time: 15 minutes
Baking Time: 50 minutes
Oven Temperature: 350°

3 whole chicken breasts, split
  and skinned (about 2 lbs.)
1 tsp. salt
1/8 tsp. black pepper
1 can (10½-oz.) condensed
  mushroom soup

½ cup canned tomatoes, snipped
  and drained and sweetened with
2 tsp. sugar
3 Tbsp. dry white wine
½ tsp. rosemary leaves, crumbled
1 jar (3½-oz.) cocktail onions,
  drained

Season chicken with a blend of salt and pepper. Arrange in 13 x 9 x 2" baking pan. Mix remaining ingredients in a bowl and pour over chicken breasts. Bake at 350° about 50 minutes or until chicken is tender, basting occasionally with sauce in dish.

Clare Joy

Chicken Divine

Easy

Serves: 4 to 6

Preparation Time: 30 minutes
Cooking Time: 1 hour
Oven Temperature: 350°

1 pkg. frozen broccoli spears,
  defrosted
4 chicken thighs
4 chicken breasts
1 can cream of mushroom soup

½ cup Miracle Whip
½ tsp. lemon juice
¼ tsp. curry powder
1 cup grated sharp cheese

Combine soup, Miracle Whip, lemon juice, and curry powder. Lay chicken pieces on bottom of glass baking pan, lay broccoli on top of chicken. Pour soup mixture over chicken and broccoli. Sprinkle cheese over soup. Bake 1 hour at 350°, or until chicken feels done when pierced with fork.

Carol Yearsley

Easy Orangey Chicken

Easy

Serves: 4

Marinate: Overnight
Preparation Time: 15 minutes
Baking Time: 1½ hours
Oven Temperature: 350°

1 frying chicken, cut up
1 small can frozen orange juice,
  undiluted

1 bottle Miracle French Dressing
1 small jar red currant jelly (10-oz.)

Marinate chicken in French dressing overnight in refrigerator. Turn once or twice. Pour off marinade and arrange chicken parts on baking dish. Blend juice and jelly over low heat, just until jelly melts. Pour over chicken and cover; bake at 350°, 1½ hours. Uncover last part of cooking time and brown to your preference, being mindful not to burn.

Jane Skeoch

Chicken-Rice Casserole

Easy

Serves: 4 to 6

Preparation Time: 5 to 10 minutes
Cooking Time: 1 hour and 15 minutes
Oven Temperature: 350°

1½ cut up chickens
6 Tbsp. margarine
1 cup uncooked rice
1 Tbsp. dry onion soup mix

3 cans soup:
  Golden Mushroom
  Cream of Vegetable
  Cream of Chicken
(or substitute Cream of Celery or
other cream soup)

Melt margarine in 9 x 13" pan. Mix rice and soup and put in pan. Arrange chicken on top of rice and soup. Bake about 1 hour and 15 minutes in a 350° oven.

Kay King

Curried Chicken

This is a good dish to serve buffet style for a group, increasing recipe!

Average
Serves: 8

Preparation Time: 45 minutes
Cooking Time: 1 ½ hours

1½ cut-up chickens (I use breasts, legs, thighs, and wings)
½ cup flour
2 Tbsp. curry powder
2 tsp. salt
oil

10 cups water
1 Tbsp. curry powder
½ cup flour
2 Tbsp. curry powder
1 cup water

CONDIMENTS:
2 tomatoes
2 bananas
½ cup chopped nuts
2 cups bread cubes
1 cup coconut

3 boiled eggs
2 cups raisins
1 jar chutney
rice

Remove skin from chicken. Mix ½ cup flour and 2 Tbsp. curry powder, 2 tsp. salt. Roll chicken pieces in this and brown in skillet with just enough oil to keep from sticking. After chicken is browned, transfer to large stew pot. Add 10 cups water, 1 Tbsp. curry powder, and bring to boil. Reduce heat and simmer for 1 hour or until tender. Take flour and curry mixture that was left after browning; add ½ cup flour, 2 Tbsp. curry powder. Mix with 1 cup water to make thickening, stirring constantly. When thickened, return chicken to pot and cook ½ hour longer. Serve over rice. Put condiments on top and eat together.

CONDIMENTS: Dice tomatoes, chop nuts, chop eggs fine, slice the bananas last as they darken. In skillet with oil, heat raisins, they will puff. Brown bread cubes in oil. Place all condiments in individual bowls.

Jo Case

Turkey Tetrazinni

So easy for a crowd!!

Average

Serves: 8 to 10

Preparation Time: 30 minutes
Cooking Time: 30 minutes
Oven Temperature: 350°

1 can cream of mushroom soup
1 can cream of chicken soup
1 cup turkey broth
2 cups grated cheese
6 cups cooked spaghetti
   (12 oz. uncooked)

4 cups diced turkey, cooked
½ cup mushrooms or toasted
   almonds
½ cup cooked, chopped onion
½ cup cooked, chopped celery
½ cup grated Parmesan cheese

Mix all ingredients except Parmesan cheese. Sprinkle grated Parmesan cheese on top. Bake for 30 minutes in a 350° oven.

Jennifer Clark

Stuffed Chicken Roma

Takes a bit of watching, especially during the first 10 minutes cooking period to make sure the fire does not flare up and burn the chicken. However, the results are certainly worth it. (If there is any butter left over, do not baste chicken during cooking time.)

Average
Serves: 6

Preparation Time: 40 minutes
Cooking Time: 40 minutes

3 whole chicken breasts
   split and boned
2 Tbsp. of green onion, chopped

1½ cups fresh bread crumbs
¼ lb. soft salami, diced
½ cup butter

Saute onion in three tablespoons butter and add the bread crumbs and diced salami. Divide the stuffing among the six pieces of chicken. Roll the breasts so that no stuffing can escape and secure with toothpicks. Melt remaining butter and allow breasts to marinate in the butter until fire is ready. Grill over charcoal approximately eight inches above the flame for forty minutes. This allows ten minutes on each of the four sides.

Judy Montgomery

Marmalade Duck

The duck cooks overnight which defats it and leaves the skin crisp and delicious.

Easy

Serves: 2 to 3

Preparation Time: 15 minutes
First Baking: Overnight
Second Baking: 40 minutes

1 Long Island duckling
salt
pepper
1 tsp. rosemary

1 cup chopped celery tops
1 cup seedless grapes
1 cup orange marmalade
3 Tbsp. curacao or orange liquer

Preheat oven to 200°. Stuff duck with celery and grapes, sprinkling inside and out with salt and pepper. Sprinkle rosemary on outside of duck. Place duck on rack in roasting pan. Roast overnight (about 11 hours) at 200°. In the morning remove duck and wrap in foil. Put in a cool place. In the evening remove foil and put the duck in a 400° oven for about 30 minutes or until it begins to brown. Then smear with orange marmalade mixed with the liquer and continue baking until nicely browned.

Marge D'Atri

Quick Turkey Curry

Easy
Serves: 4

Preparation Time: 15 minutes
Cooking Time: 15 minutes

¼ cup onion, chopped
1 can condensed cream of
    mushroom soup
1 cup dairy sour cream
1 cup turkey, cooked and cubed

1 Tbsp. margarine
¼ cup milk
1 tsp. curry powder, or more
    to taste
parsley

Cook onion in margarine. Add soup and milk; heat and stir until smooth, stir in sour cream and curry powder. Add turkey; and heat. Garnish with snipped parsley. Serve over hot cooked rice. Offer curry condiments: chutney, raisins, toasted slivered almonds, coconut, and sliced green onion.

Clare Joy

Hawaiian Chicken

Easy
Serves: 4 to 5

Preparation Time: 10 minutes

2 cups cooked chicken (turkey or
  tuna substitute very nicely)
1 clove garlic, minced
1 green pepper, sliced
2 tsp. soy sauce

2 cans soup, mushroom or any
  cream soup
1 can chunk pineapple, including
  the juice

Saute garlic and green pepper. Add soup and pineapple, mix and heat. (We like this with chunks of chicken that have been stewing in the crock pot all day!!) Add tuna or chicken and soy sauce. Serve with rice.

Kay King

Stuffed Chicken Thighs

Complicated
Serves: 8

Preparation Time: 45 minutes
Cooking Time: 30 minutes

8 chicken thighs (8 oz. each)
2 lbs. pork sausage
1⅓ cups cooked rice
1 lb. mushrooms, sliced
butter, for frying

several Tbsp. Cointreau
⅓ cup Madeira wine
4 Tbsp. brown sugar
1 orange, juiced
salt and pepper to taste

Make stuffing by combining sausage, rice, mushrooms, wine, salt, and pepper. Stuff mixture into pocket of each thigh, between skin and flesh, and tie off both ends of thigh with string. Brown thighs in frying pan with butter. Then remove the thigh and set aside on a warm platter. Deglaze the pan with Cointreau and orange juice. Put chicken back in the pan. Cover and cook for 30 more minutes over medium heat.

Alice Glass

SEAFOOD

Beer Batter Fish Fry

Average

Serves: 12

Preparation Time: 10 minutes
Refrigeration Time: 3 to 12 hour
Deep Fat Fry Temperature: 375°

2 eggs, separated
1 cup flat beer
1 Tbsp. butter, melted

1⅓ cups flour
½ tsp. salt
dash pepper

Beat 2 egg yolks. Add 1 cup of flat beer, 1 Tbsp. melted butter, salt and pepper. Stir into 1⅓ cups of flour. Refrigerate the batter for 3 to 12 hours. When ready to fry the fish, add 2 fluffy beaten egg whites to the batter, folding in gently. Pat fish filets dry with paper towels. Dredge lightly with flour, dip in batter. Deep fry at 375° for 3 to 5 minutes depending on size of fillet.

Eunice Braman

Crab and Shrimp with Rice

Easy

Serves: 4 to 6

Preparation Time: 15 minutes
Baking Time: 1 hour
Oven Temperature: 350°

1½ lbs. crabmeat -OR
  2 cans crab
½ lb. small shrimp
½ green pepper, chopped
⅓ cup parsley, chopped

2 cups cooked rice
1½ cups mayonnaise
2 pkgs. frozen peas, thawed
salt and white pepper to taste

Toss lightly. Place in a greased casserole; refrigerate, covered. Bake one hour at 350° covered. (A shallow dish is best.)

Jane Skeoch

Coquilles St. Jacques

*Can do ahead and freeze! Such a hit, I make double the recipe.
So elegant, guests will go wild over this one!! So will husbands!*

Average

Serves: 6

Preparation Time: 30 to 45 minutes
Cooking Time: 15 minutes
Broiler Time: 5 minutes

1½ lbs scallops
1½ cups *dry* white wine
½ tsp. salt
¼ tsp. white pepper
¼ cup fresh mushrooms,
  coarsely chopped

3 Tbsp. butter
2 Tbsp. flour
1 cup milk
2 Tbsp. bread crumbs
green onion, chopped
3 Tbsp. Swiss Cheese

Combine scallops, wine, salt, and pepper in heavy sauce-pan; bring slowly to a boil. Simmer 5 minutes. Drain off liquid and set aside*! Cut scallops in small pieces. Make white sauce from butter, milk, and flour, and liquid* from scallops. Cook 3 minutes stirring constantly. Add scallops and mushrooms. Cook 5 minutes, stirring occasionally. Remove from fire, add cheese and seasonings. Fill buttered *shells* or small individual oven-proof (crock type) dishes. Top with bread crumbs. Put under broiler until bubbly or freeze for use later.

Grace Berg

Poached Fish

This can be an appetizer, fish course, or main course.

Complicated

Preparation Time: 10 minutes
Cooking Time: 50 minutes

4 cups water
2 cups dry white wine
1 carrot, sliced
1 stalk celery, sliced
1 small onion, sliced
1 lemon, sliced
2 sprigs parsley

2 bay leaves
½ tsp. tarragon
½ tsp. thyme
1 Tbsp. salt
4 peppercorns
1 large fish or filets about
    three lbs.

Mix first 12 ingredients in large saucepan. Boil covered for about 20 minutes. Strain and place liquid in poacher or skillet. Clean fish then wrap in cheesecloth. Place in lukewarm poaching liquid. The liquid (Court bouillon) should cover the fish. If it does not, add enough water to cover. Cover skillet or poacher and simmer for about 15 minutes. Remove from heat and let fish sit in liquid for another 15 minutes. Then lift out of liquid by ends of cheesecloth. Remove cheesecloth and arrange whole fish or fillets on platter. Surround with lemon slices and parsley. Serve warm or cold with your favorite sauce. I prefer to serve it warm with a Hollandaise or Beurre Blanc sauce.

BEURRE BLANC SAUCE:

Preparation Time: 20 minutes

⅓ cup white wine vinegar
⅓ cup dry white wine
2 Tbsp. finely chopped green
    onions

½ tsp. salt
1/8 tsp. white pepper
½ lb. butter, cut into 16 pieces
    and thoroughly chilled

In saucepan, bring first five ingredients to a boil over high heat. Cook uncovered stirring occasionally until liquid is reduced to about one tablespoon. Remove from heat and with a wire whisk *immediately* whip in three pieces of butter. Return pan to lowest heat and whip each piece of butter in separately until all is absorbed. The finished sauce will be thick and ivory-colored. Serve at once.

Robin Lightner

Poached Trout

When poached, it is delicious cold—plain or with tartar sauce.

Average
Serves: 6 to 8

Preparation Time: 1 hour
Poaching Time: 10 to 15 minutes

8 cups water
1 carrot, chunked
6 peppercorns
2 tsp. salt
1 Tbsp. lemon juice or vinegar

1 onion, sliced
2 stalks celery, diced
4 cloves
1 bay leaf
4 lbs. cleaned trout

Bring stock to boil, simmer for ½ hour, let cool for ½ hour, strain. To poach fish—use poacher or trivet in pan. Grease pan, place fish in pan, can be wrapped in cheesecloth. Bring stock to boil, pour over fish. Cover pan, put in hot oven (425°) for 10 minutes per pound, or simmer on top of stove until fish flakes when tested—10 to 15 minutes. Serve with Hollandaise sauce or fish sauce.

FISH SAUCE: Melt three tablespoons of butter or oleo. Stir in three tablespoons of flour, add two cups of fish stock. Salt and pepper if needed, a dash of nutmeg for variation or add chopped egg, dillweed, capers, mushrooms. One-half cup of wine is also good. Sprinkle with parsley and serve. This fish is equally good served hot or cold.

Mildred Buchenroth
Sandy Bommer

Trout Sauteed in Butter

Average
Serves: 4

Preparation Time: 10 to 15 minutes
Cooking Time: 12 minutes

11 Tbsp. butter (¼ lb. plus 3 Tbsp.)
salt
flour
1 Tbsp. oil
4 Tbsp. finely chopped fresh
    parsley

4 whole fresh ½ lb. trout -OR-
    defrosted frozen trout, cleaned
    but with heads and tails left on
2 Tbsp. lemon juice

In a 1½ to 2 quart saucepan, clarify 8 tablespoons of the butter by melting it slowly, skimming off the surface foam. Spoon the clear butter on top into a 6 to 8 inch skillet and discard the milky solids at the bottom of the pan. Set aside.

Wash trout under cold running water and dry them completely with paper towels. Season them inside and out with salt, dip them into flour and then shake them to remove all but a light dusting of the flour. In a heavy 10 to 12 inch skillet, melt the remaining three tablespoons of butter with the oil over moderately high heat. When the foam subsides, add trout and saute them over high heat, turning them with kitchen tongs for 5 or 6 minutes on each side, or until they are of a golden color and just firm when pressed lightly with a finger. Transfer trout to a heated platter and cover lightly to keep warm.

Cook the clarified butter over low heat until it browns lightly. Do not let it burn. Sprinkle the trout with lemon juice and parsley, pour the hot butter over them and serve immediately.

Beth McKee

Salmon and Broccoli Casserole

Average

Serves: 4

Preparation Time: 30 minutes
Baking Time: 25 minutes
Oven Temperature: 375°

2 pkgs. frozen broccoli spears
1 large can salmon (16 oz.)
4 Tbsp. butter
3 tsp. minced garlic
5 Tbsp. flour

juice from canned salmon, plus
   enough milk to make 1½ cups
¾ cup sharp Cheddar cheese,
   grated
1 can tomatoes (16 oz.)
buttered bread crumbs for topping, if desired

    Spray casserole with "Pam." Flake drained salmon and put in casserole. Cook broccoli spears one half the length of time recommended on package. Arrange broccoli spears on top of salmon. Saute garlic in butter, add flour and stir in juice and milk. Continue stirring and cooking until sauce thickens and boils. Add cheese and tomatoes. Pour over broccoli spears and salmon. Sprinkle with buttered bread crumbs. Bake at 375° for 25 minutes or until hot and bubbly.

Marsha Holden

Shrimp and Cheese Dish

Average
Serves: 4 to 6

Preparation Time: 20 minutes

¼ cup butter
½ cup chopped green pepper
¼ cup flour
2 cups milk
1 cup shredded sharp Cheddar
   cheese
¾ lb. cooked shrimp cut in halves

chow mein noodles or toasted
   English muffins
1 tsp. salt
1 tsp. Worcestershire sauce
¼ tsp. dry mustard
¼ tsp. paprika
½ tsp. dill weed

Cook green pepper in butter for five minutes. Stir in flour. Gradually add the milk. Cook over medium heat until thickened, stirring constantly. Add cheese, salt, Worcestershire sauce, dry mustard, paprika, dill weed, and shrimp. Heat until cheese melts and mixture is hot. Serve over noodles or toasted muffins.

Ann Dankert

Shrimp Creole

A delicious luncheon or supper dish.

Easy
Serves: 4

Preparation Time: 45 minutes

¼ diced green pepper
½ cup diced celery
½ cup diced onion
1 Tbsp. flour
½ tsp. salt, dash of pepper
½ tsp. Lea & Perrins
¾ lbs. cleaned, cooked shrimp

3 Tbsp. butter
1 ¾ cups canned tomatoes
1 tsp. sugar
1 bay leaf
small sprig of parsley
1⅓ cups minute rice

Saute green pepper, onion, and celery in butter until tender. Add flour and blend. Add tomatoes gradually. Stir constantly. Add salt, pepper, sugar, bay leaf, and parsley. Cook gently for 30 minutes. Remove bay leaf and parsley. Add shrimp and Lea & Perrins and heat through. Prepare minute rice as directed on package. Serve shrimp creole over rice.

Marge D'Atri

Golden Shrimp Casserole

Super recipe to make ahead, it refrigerates and freezes well!!

Average

Serves: 4

Preparation Time: 30 minutes
Baking Time: 50 to 60 minutes
Oven Temperature: 325°

8 slices bread, dried, trimmed,
　buttered, and cubed
2 cups shrimp, frozen or canned
1 cup mushrooms, drained
2 cups (½ lb.) sharp cheese,
　shredded
½ tsp. salt
3 eggs

½ tsp. dry mustard
2 cups milk
dash of lemon juice
dash of paprika
dash of Worcestershire sauce
dash of Accent

　　Put half of bread cubes in greased baking dish, 9" x 9". add shrimp, mushrooms, and half of cheese. Then add the rest of bread and top with cheese. Beat eggs and add seasonings and milk. Pour over top. Bake in slow oven of 325° for 50 to 60 minutes. May place a pan of water in the oven.

Kathy Phillips

ACCOMPANIMENTS

Blender Hollandaise

This is really "Never Fail"!!

Easy   *Preparation Time: 10 minutes*
Yield: 1 cup

1 stick butter   ¼ tsp. salt
3 egg yolks   few grains of cayenne pepper
2 tsp. lemon juice

Heat butter until it bubbles. In blender, put egg yolks and lemon juice, salt and cayenne. Cover and turn on then off immediately. Put blender on high and pour butter very gradually into mixture. To keep warm set in pan of warm water.

Robin Lightner

Fried Apples

A very good accompaniment to game.

Easy   *Preparation Time: 30 minutes*
Serves: 4

4 large firm apples, cored and   1 large onion, sliced thin
   sliced ¼ inch thick   3 Tbsp. sugar
1½ Tbsp. butter   ½ tsp. lemon juice

Melt butter in skillet and saute onion and apple. Sprinkle with sugar and lemon juice. Cover and cook over low heat for 10 to 15 minutes or until apples are tender.

Robin Lightner

Fresh Salsa Picante (Taco Sauce)

This is different from the usual taco sauce because you use fresh tomatoes.

Easy
Yield: 3 cups

Preparation Time: 20 minutes
Refrigeration Time: 6 hours

4 firm ripe tomatoes
1 4-oz. can Ortegas chopped
   green chilies
1 medium onion, chopped
1 clove garlic, minced

¼ tsp. salt
dash of pepper
2 Tbsp. vinegar
5 drops Tabasco sauce, or more
   if desired

Peel and chop tomatoes and put in blender. Add onions and garlic and chilies. Whirl until pulverized. Stir in salt, pepper, vinegar, and Tabasco sauce. Let stand for several hours to blend flavor. Use as a sauce for tacos or serve with fried or scrambled eggs. It is also excellent served with broiled steak.

Marge D'Atri

Chutney/Red Currant Sauce

Easy
Yield: About 2 cups

Preparation Time: 10 minutes

1 9-oz. jar chutney
1 10-oz. jar red currant jelly
slosh of brandy (if desired) or
   lemon juice

In top of double boiler, blend chutney and jelly, till well blended and heated through. Add brandy or lemon juice and stir. Excellent with ham for a glaze or served warm in a pretty dish to be used at table.

Jane Skeoch

Tartar Sauce

Marvelous with any fried fish.

Easy　　　　　　　　　　　　*Preparation Time: 15 minutes*
Yield: 3 cups

15 stuffed green olives
1 medium onion chopped, or
　6 green onions, chopped
1 whole large dill pickle, chopped
1 cup mayonnaise (Hellmans or
　Best Foods)

½ cup sour cream
½ lemon, squeezed
2 tsp. dill weed
¼ tsp. salt
¼ tsp. pepper

Chop olives, onion, and pickle very finely. Add mayonnaise, sour cream and seasonings.

Ellie Wiegand

Horseradish Sauce

Easy　　　　　　　　　　　　*Preparation Time: 10 minutes*
Yield: 1 ½ cups

½ cup heavy cream
¼ cup lemon juice

2 to 3 Tbsp. prepared horseradish
dash of salt and paprika

Whip cream until it is quite stiff; continue beating while adding lemon juice, horseradish, salt and paprika. Very good with roast beef!

Jane Skeoch

Hot Mustard Sauce

This is delicious with raw vegetables as a dip or use it as a dressing with cold turkey, ham, or beef.

Easy
Yield: 3 cups

Preparation Time: 12 hours

1 cup dry mustard
3 eggs
1 cup sour cream

1 cup vinegar
1 cup sugar

   Combine dry mustard with vinegar and allow to stand over night. Beat three (3) eggs in the top of double boiler, add one cup sugar and the mustard mixture. Cook over simmering water until thick and smooth. Cool and combine with one cup of sour cream.

Ellen Dornan (Mrs. Jack Dornan)

Teri-Yaki Marinade for Chicken

This is an excellent marinade for any teri-yaki dish.

Easy

Yield: 1 cup

Preparation Time: 5 minutes
Marinating Time: 1 hour
Baking Time: 1 hour
Oven Temperature: 350°

⅔ cup soy sauce
⅓ cup white wine
1 clove garlic, minced

2 Tbsp. sugar
½ tsp. ginger

   Mix together all ingredients and marinate one cut-up fryer or split broiler for one hour. Bake in 350° oven for one hour. Baste frequently with the marinade.

Marge D'Atri

WILD GAME

John Clymer
'78

WILD GAME

The wide open spaces and the great out-of-doors which our lives evolve around, is the big attraction that holds most of the people here in the valley. Many live for the thrills of the hunting season. Hunting talk can be heard year round, along the streets, in the bars, and in the supermarkets. But mostly in the fall the question is: "Have you got your meat yet??!!"

There are many exotic ways of preparing wild game into an epicurean's delight, but for those who eat wild game on a regular basis, it must be easy and quick to prepare, yet moist, tender, and flavorful. Keeping it simple is a good rule that will be appreciated by gourmet and cook alike. Bon appetit!!!!

Beth McKee

Belgium Summer Sausage

Good served as hors d'oeuvres.

Average

Preparation Time: 30 minutes
Refrigeration Time: 3 days

Yield: 5 rolls

Oven Time: 7½ hours at 150°

5 lbs. ground venison or lean beef
5 Tbsp. Morton's tender quick salt
2½ Tbsp. coarse ground pepper

2½ Tbsp. mustard seed
1 Tbsp. hickory smoke salt
2 Tbsp. garlic salt

Blend together all seasonings and then mix in ground meat, making sure spices are evenly distributed. Cover and refrigerate for 3 days, kneading the mixture once each day. Roll into 5 tight rolls about 2 inches in diameter. Place on broiler pan and bake at 150° for 7½ hours.

Jennie Tipton

Venison or Elk Empanadas
(Little Meat Pies)

Empanadas are better if made and frozen before cooking. They are crisper and saltier, otherwise more salt needs to be added.

Average

Yield: 36 empanadas

Preparation Time: 45 minutes
Oven Time: 15 minutes
Oven Temperature: 375° to 400°

DOUGH:
1 cup butter
2 (8 oz.) pkgs. cream cheese
2 cups flour
½ tsp. salt
paprika

FILLING:
1 lb. ground elk or venison
1 onion, chopped fine
1 Tbsp. flour
dash of Tabasco
1 Tbsp. Worcestershire sauce
1 tsp. chili powder, or to taste
salt and pepper to taste
¼ cup red wine

Soften butter and cream cheese. Using mixer, blend until smooth. Add flour and salt. Blend. Divide into 2 balls and refrigerate. Meanwhile, make fillings: Brown ground meat. Add rest of ingredients, after draining excess fat, and cook thoroughly. After dough is chilled, on a lightly floured board, roll 1 ball to about 1/8 inch thickness. Cut out circles with large biscuit cutter or small bowl or glass. Place small amount of filling on half of each circle. Moisten edges with water. Fold in half and crimp edges with fork. Sprinkle with paprika. Bake at 375° to 400° for 15 minutes or until golden brown. Serve warm.

Robin Lightner

Elk Sirloin Au Roquefort

If you like Roquefort, you will love the taste of this steak.

Easy　　　　　　　　　　*Marinate Time: 1 hour or more*
　　　　　　　　　　　　　Preparation Time: 5 minutes
Yield: 6 servings　　*Cooking Time: 16 minutes for medium rare*

large sirloin steak, cut
　1½ inches thick
2 Tbsp. crumbled Roquefort
　cheese

2 Tbsp. salad oil
1 Tbsp. lemon juice
fresh ground pepper

　　Spread above mixture on both sides of steak, allow to stand one hour or more. Prepare coals. Grill steak five inches from coals, eight minutes per side for medium rare. Turn once. Sprinkle top with additional Roquefort, crumbled, and a bit of parsley, minced. Salt the steak after it comes to the table.

Ellen Dornan (Mrs. Jack Dornan)

Elk or Deer Tenderloin Rotel

Easy　　　　　　　　　*Preparation Time: 10 minutes*
Serves: 6 to 8　　　　　*Cooking Time: 20 minutes*

3 to 4 lbs. elk or deer tenderloin
3 Tbsp. oil

salt and pepper to taste
1 can Rotel tomatoes with green
　chilies

　　Slice tenderloin ¼ to ½ inch thick across the grain. Brown in a heavy skillet in oil. Add salt and pepper to taste. Add Rotel tomatoes, mashing to blend. Continue cooking until tenderloins are tender, about 15 to 20 minutes.

Judy Barbour
from her book,
Elegant Elk, Delicious Deer

Elk/Antelope/Deer Loin Roast

Average

Preparation Time: 40 minutes
Cooking Time: 1 ¼ hours

1 large OR 2 small loins
8 pitted prunes
1 large peeled, sliced apple
½ cup butter OR ¼ cup butter
   and ¼ cup oil

3 slices bacon
20 small white onions
½ cup cognac
1 cup white wine
salt and pepper

Split loin and lay flat. Sprinkle with salt and pepper. Lay prunes and sliced apple into loin. Add some butter and the bacon slices. Use toothpicks to join sides and tie with string making a roll. Melt remaining butter or oil in a heavy Dutch oven. Brown meat on all sides. After it is well browned, add the small white onions. Pour cognac over meat and flame, moving pan so that the cognac flames over all the meat. When flames die down, add one cup of white wine. Cover and simmer for 1¼ hours over medium low heat.

SAUCE:

2 Tbsp. red currant jelly

¼ cup heavy cream

Pour sauce from cooked meat into a saucepan. Boil down a bit. Add 2 Tbsp. red currant jelly and the heavy cream. Simmer to thicken. Slice meat. Place onions around meat and pour sauce over meat and onions.

Rosemary Laumeyer

Elk Wellington

Very elegant and very impressive.

Average

Serves: 4

Preparation Time: 25 minutes
Cooking Time: 20 to 30 minutes
Oven Temperature: 425°

1 elk back strap (filet)
1 can pate de fois gras

1 recipe of your favorite pastry

Pepper back strap generously. Brown well on all sides in bacon grease. Set aside and let cool. Roll out the pastry into a rectangle about 2½ inches longer than the back strap. Place cool back strap in center of pastry. Spread pate on one side, turn over and spread rest of pate on the other side of meat. Bring pastry up around meat. Moisten edges and seal. Moisten ends and seal. Place on cookie sheet. Any left over pastry can be rolled out and used to decorate top. Preheat oven to 425°. Bake until pastry is brown, about 20 to 30 minutes. The meat should be medium rare to medium. Serve with bernaise sauce or bordelaise sauce.

It is hard to tell exactly how long to cook this as each back strap is different in size. If it is larger than 3 inches thick, reduce the oven temperature a bit and cook a little longer. If it is skinnier, a higher temperature and shorter cooking time will brown the pastry without overcooking the meat.

Robin Lightner

Meat Ball Kabobs

Sauce is great for barbequing chicken also.

Easy   *Preparation Time: 30 minutes*
Serves: 6 to 8   *Baking Time: 30 minutes*

2 lbs. ground meat
  (beef, elk, deer, or moose)
2 tsp. salt
½ tsp. coarse black pepper
¾ tsp. monosodium glutamate
18 to 24 large pimento stuffed
  olives

1 bunch of green onion, cut in
  1½ inch pieces
12 to 16 cherry tomatoes
⅓ cup olive oil
1 clove garlic, crushed
hard rolls

Toss together meat, salt, pepper, and monosodium glutamate. Form into 18 to 24 meat balls about 1½ inches in
diameter. Press each meat ball together firmly on 6 or 8 metal
skewers, arrange olives, green onions, and tomatoes. Mix oil
and garlic, then brush onto kabobs. Grill to desired doneness,
turning once. Serve with Hot Olive Barbeque Sauce on rolls.

OLIVE BARBEQUE SAUCE:

⅓ cup vinegar
½ cup firmly packed brown sugar
1/8 tsp. salt
¾ cup catsup

1 tsp. soy sauce
1 tsp. prepared mustard
1 12-oz. can unsweetened pineapple juice
½ cup chopped pimento stuffed
  olives

Mix all ingredients, except olives, in saucepan. Boil, stirring occasionally, then simmer uncovered for 30 minutes. Stir
in olives. Makes 2½ cups.

Fran Johnson

Hunters' Venison Steaks

Average
Serves: 6

Marinate Time: 4 to 24 hours
Cooking Time: 15 minutes

6 ¾" thick steaks from elk or deer
¼ cup white wine
2 tsp. butter
2 shallots or green onion
1 Tbsp. flour
1 cup sour cream
lemon juice

MARINADE:
4 peppercorns
1 onion
1 carrot
4 sprigs parsley
½ tsp. thyme
1 bay leaf
½ cup white wine
5 tsp. oil

To make marinade: crush peppercorns, slice onion and carrot, add parsley, thyme, bay leaf, white wine and oil. Pour over steak and marinate from four to twenty-four hours.

Saute steaks in 3 Tbsp. oil over high heat for about three minutes on each side, remove from pan and keep warm. Drain excess fat from cooking pan and to remaining juices add two Tbsp. butter and two shallots, minced. Add 1 Tbsp. flour and cook until roux is slightly brown. Add the wine and pepper to taste and sour cream. Cook stirring constantly until sauce is smooth and thick. Correct seasoning with salt and lemon juice and pour over steaks.

Judy Montgomery

Chicken Fried Elk or Venison with Cream Gravy

My husband's favorite elk or venison. Tender and yummy!

Easy   *Preparation Time: 20 minutes*
Serves: 6   *Cooking Time: 30 minutes*

3 lbs. venison or elk (any cut as   oil or shortening
   long as the steaks contain no   salt and pepper to taste
   bone)   garlic powder to taste
1 can cream of mushroom soup
1 can milk
½ can water

    Steaks should be about 2 inches thick. Pound with meat mallet until it looks like a cutlet. Soak cutlets in milk for about 10 minutes. Mix flour, salt, pepper, and garlic powder. Dust meat in flour mixture. Fry in hot oil until golden brown. Remove to platter and keep warm. Pour off excess fat in skillet, leaving a couple of tablespoons of fat. Add two tablespoons of flour. Make a roux and brown. Add 1 can of mushroom soup, 1 can of milk and ½ can of water. Correct seasonings. Stir until gravy thickens, if too thick, thin with milk. Serve with cutlets. Mashed potatoes or rice go well with gravy. If you're not a gravy freak, a squeeze of lemon juice over cutlets is good. You may also add wine to gravy.

Robin Lightner

Elk Meatloaf

Easy

Serves: 6 to 8

Preparation Time: 20 minutes
Cooking Time: 1 ½ hours
Oven Temperature: 350°

2 lbs. of ground elk
1½ cups cracker crumbs
    (Saltines or Ritz)
½ onion, chopped
¼ cup milk

2 eggs
¼ cup catsup
dash of Worcestershire sauce
salt and pepper
garlic powder (several dashes)

Mix eggs, milk, catsup, Worcestershire sauce in a small bowl or cup. Beat. Meanwhile, mix ground meat, cracker crumbs, salt, pepper, and garlic powder and onion. Pour liquid over and blend thoroughly. Bake at 350° for 1½ hours. Serve with sauce. Also good with just gravy.

SAUCE:

1 can tomato sauce
2 heaping Tbsp. catsup

2 Tbsp. instant onion
1 Tbsp. parsley

Mix all ingredients, heat and serve.

Robin Lightner

Venison or Elk Parmigiana

Easy

Serves: 4

Preparation Time: 10 minutes
Cooking Time: 20 minutes
Oven Temperature: 400°

2 lbs. boneless deer, elk, or ante-
    lope steaks, cut ½ inch thick
flour

3 cups spaghetti sauce
½ lb. mozzarella cheese, grated
Parmesan cheese

Dredge steaks in flour. Saute quickly in hot oil just until brown. Place in heat-proof serving dish in one layer. Cover with spaghetti sauce and sprinkle the mozzarella cheese over it. Then sprinkle with Parmesan cheese. Bake in 400° oven for 10 to 15 minutes. The trick is to cook the meat just until it is medium. Overcooking game toughens it.

Marge D'Atri

Venison Cutlets

I use the sauce for a dip for venison roast at parties and it is always a success.

Average   *Preparation Time: Approximately 30 minutes*
Serves: 6

	SAUCE:
3 lbs. venison steaks, cut from	1 egg separated
the loin	¾ cup melted butter
salt and pepper to taste	2 tsp. sour pickle, chopped
½ cup butter, melted	1 tsp. onion, chopped
bread crumbs	2 tsp. lemon juice

Sprinkle steaks with salt and pepper. Take a few bread crumbs and pour melted butter over the crumbs. Bathe the steaks with the melted butter and crumbs and fry or broil the meat to a rare, medium or well done stage, depending on the individual taste.

SAUCE:

Add the finely chopped pickle, onion (which has been finely chopped), and the lemon juice to the melted butter. Separate the egg and add only the yolk; beat the egg whites stiff and add to the mixture. Pour over cutlets and serve.

Beth McKee

Marinated Venison Stew

I am told that if you add one half pint of rum and a half dozen strawberries, it will taste like boiled strawberry daquiri and will "soothe the savage beast," and will be conducive to some peaceful rest.

Complicated   *Preparation Time: 45 minutes*
Yield: 6 servings   *Cooking Time: 2 hours*

Cut 3 lbs. of meat into 1½   10 peppercorns
    inch cubes   5 juniper berries, crushed
2 medium onions, sliced   1 Tbsp. parsley, chopped
2 stalks celery, chopped   1 bay leaf
1 carrot, sliced   juice of 1 lemon
1 clove garlic, crushed   1 16-oz. bottle or can of beer
1 tsp. salt   ½ cup salad oil

Combine marinade and pour over meat in a large earthenware bowl and let stand a couple of days in the refrigerator, turning meat several times. Place meat and marinade in a large pot and bring slowly to a boil. Cover and cook over low heat a couple of hours. Remove meat and strain liquid, forcing vegetables through the strainer.

Eunice Braman

Zesty Meat Pies

Here's one where you can use game meat as well as beef!!!

Average

Serves: 7 small pies

Preparation Time: 20 minutes
Cooking Time: 25 minutes
Oven Temperature: 400°

1 3-oz. pkg. cream cheese,
  softened
1⅓ cups unsifted flour
1 lb. ground meat, your choice
1 egg, slightly beaten

½ cup butter -OR- margarine,
  softened
½ tsp. salt
¾ cup undrained hamburger
  relish
1 tsp. water

Combine cheese, butter, flour, and one-half teaspoon of salt. Mix with pastry blender or cut into mixture with two knives until very fine particles form. Form dough into ball. Wrap in waxed paper and refrigerate until chilled. Crumble the meat into heated skillet. Cook over moderate heat until meat loses red color. Break up meat in small pieces with edge of spoon. Combine meat, one teaspoon salt, pepper, and hamburger relish. Mix well. Pinch off about a fourth of the dough at a time (keep remainder refrigerated while working with it) and roll dough to about 1/8 inch thickness. Cut into 14 circles each about four and one-half inches in diameter. Spoon 1/4 cup of meat mixture onto center of each of seven pastry circles. Top with remaining pastry circles. Moisten edges of bottom pastry with water. Crimp edges with fork to seal. Mix together egg and water. Brush tops of pastry circles with mixture. Place on a lightly greased baking sheet. Bake in oven preheated to 400° about 25 minutes or until pastry is golden brown. Serve hot or cold. Meat pies may be frozen and packed in lunch box.

Anna L. Scrivens

Venison Parmesan

Easy

Serves: 4

Preparation Time: 30 minutes
Baking Time: 1 hour
Oven Temperature: 350°

1½ lbs. venison
flour
Parmesan cheese, grated
4 Tbsp. butter
3 Tbsp. olive oil

1 onion, chopped
1 green pepper, chopped
1 cup boiling water
1 beef bouillon cube
¼ cup red wine

Cut venison into strips ½" by 2" size. Mix equal parts of Parmesan cheese and flour. Roll venison in mixture. Melt butter and olive oil in skillet. Brown venison. Remove venison. If necessary, add more butter and saute onion and green pepper. Return venison to skillet and add water, bouillon cube and wine. Stir to scrape bits from bottom of pan. Cover and simmer on top of stove, or bake in oven for about 1 hour at 350° or until tender. Serve over rice or noodles.

Robin Lightner

Rolled Elk with Cranberry Stuffing

Average

Serves: 6 to 8

Preparation Time: 45 minutes
Baking Time: 2 hours and 20 minutes
Oven Temperature: 350°

1 rolled elk roast
¼ cup chopped suet
4 cups cranberries, finely
   chopped
1½ cups sugar

2 cups bread crumbs
1 Tbsp. orange rind, grated
1½ tsp. salt
¼ tsp. pepper
flour

Saute suet until crisp. Add cranberries and sugar. Cook until transparent. Add bread crumbs, orange rind, salt and pepper. Blend well and cool.

To assemble: Spread roast flat and wipe with damp towel. Sprinkle with salt and pepper. Spread with stuffing. Roll up and tie securely. Sprinkle with salt, pepper and a little flour. Sear roast in oven at 500° for about 20 minutes. Reduce heat to 350° and cook for two (2) hours or until meat thermometer reads desired doneness.

Robin Lightner

Moose Stroganoff

May also be used for venison or beef. Serve over rice or noodles.

Easy   *Preparation Time: 30 minutes*
Serves: 4 to 6   *Cooking Time: 2 hours*

1 lb. moose   ½ tsp. pepper
flour   ¼ tsp. marjoram -OR-
1 onion, sliced   ½ tsp. oregano
1 cup water   ⅓ cup catsup
1 tsp. salt   1 small can mushrooms
¾ tsp. dry mustard   ½ to 1 cup sour cream

Cut moose into finger-sized pieces. Dip into flour; brown in fat. Add onion, water, seasonings and catsup; cook over low heat for one hour. Add mushrooms; simmer for one hour longer. Add sour cream, heat for two or three minutes. I have served this to people who were skeptical of wild game and they never knew that they were eating wild game until they were told later!!

Beth McKee

Leg of Antelope

Average   *Preparation Time: 10 minutes*
                              Cooking Time: 35 minutes per pound
                                   Oven Temperature: 300°

1 leg of antelope   ½ tsp. ginger
garlic   salt and pepper
½ cup melted butter or oleo   1 can consomme
1 tsp. rosemary   ½ cup red wine
1 tsp. Worcestershire sauce

Make small slits in leg. Insert slices of garlic in slits. Add all seasonings to melted butter. Place leg of lamb in roaster. Pour melted butter over. Add salt and pepper to taste. Pour consomme and wine in bottom of pan. Bake at 300° for 35 minutes per pound. Baste with liquid frequently.

Mildred Buckenroth

Venison Pot Roast Deluxe

May be used equally well with elk or beef.

Average   *Cooking Time: Approx. 3 hours*
Yield: 8 to 10 servings

6 to 8 lb. roast
2½ cups hot water
2 bay leaves
1 clove garlic, crushed
¼ tsp. allspice
4 Tbsp. honey
4 fillets of anchovy mashed
2 Tbsp. vinegar

1 tsp. salt
fresh ground pepper
3 carrots cut in chunks
2 medium-sized onions, chopped
4 Tbsp. butter
2 cups sour cream
4 Tbsp. flour

   In a large cast iron pot (Dutch oven preferred) melt butter over medium heat. Add the roast and turn frequently until well browned. Add onions, stirring well into fat. Add the remaining ingredients, stir thoroughly and bring to a boil. Reduce heat. Simmer for 2½ hours. Remove roast to warm place. Strain the pan juices and return to pot. Stir in 2 cups of sour cream mixed with 4 Tbsp. flour. Allow to thicken but do not boil. Return roast to the sauce and simmer for 10 minutes.

Ellen Dornan (Mrs. Jack Dornan)

Pinedale Marinade for Game

Easy   *Preparation Time: 5 minutes*
Yield: 1 cup   *Marinate Meat: 1 day or more*

¾ cup soy sauce
2 Tbsp. lemon juice
6 shakes bitters
½ cup water

2 Tbsp. bourbon
½ tsp. powdered ginger
2 cloves garlic

   Mix all ingredients together. Pour over meat. Let the meat stand in the marinade for a day or longer. Turn occasionally. This is great for doing game fondue.

Boulder Lake Ranch

Venison Superb

Better when cooked a day ahead.

Average   Cooking Time: 1 to 2 hours
Serves: 4

2 lbs. venison (cut up into   3 Tbsp. bacon fat
  serving pieces)   1 cup celery, cut up
¼ cup flour   1 large onion, cut up
1 tsp. Lawry's seasoning salt   1 tsp. Worcestershire sauce
fresh ground pepper to taste   1 13-oz. can of tomatoes

Cut venison into serving pieces. Mix flour with Lawry's seasoning salt and fresh ground pepper to taste. Coat venison with flour mixture. Heat three tablespoons of bacon fat in skillet and brown venison on both sides. Add one cup celery and one large onion. Add one teaspoon of Worcestershire Sauce and tomatoes. Simmer covered one to two hours until tender. Serve with noodles. If cooked a day ahead: Butter dish and arrange noodles around side and bottom of dish. Add venison mix in center and warm up in oven at 200° for 45 minutes.

Ann Scrivens

Curried Grouse Breasts

Very good with hot biscuits or wild rice.

Average   Preparation Time: 30 minutes
Serves: 6   Cooking Time: 30 minutes

3 lbs. of grouse breasts   1 cup of sour cream
4 Tbsp. of seasoned flour   4 Tbsp. of butter
2 tsp. of curry powder   ¾ cup of consomme

Skin the breasts. Remove the bone. Roll pieces in seasoned flour. Brown in the butter in a deep skillet. Add consomme. Mix the curry powder to a paste with a little of the consomme and stir in. Cover skillet and simmer the breasts for 25 to 30 minutes, or until meltingly tender. Add sour cream (undiluted evaporated milk can be used. I have also substituted chicken broth for consomme). Pour the contents of the skillet onto a hot platter.

Beth McKee

Roast Wild Duck

A tender "non-gamy" roast duck.

Average to complicated

Serves: 4 to 6

Preparation Time: 24 hours
Cooking Time: 3 hours plus
Oven Temperature: 325°

2 to 3 whole ducks (mallards
   are best)
1 bottle red cooking wine
1 jar of cinnamon apple rings
1 bag Pepperidge Farm dressing
   mix
butter as per dressing instructions

3 stalks celery, chopped
1 or 2 medium onions, chopped
3 Tbsp. butter or margarine
1 can water chestnuts (chopped)
1 or 2 apples, chopped
1 small jar orange marmalade

Salt the body cavity of well-cleaned ducks. Marinate ducks overnight in wine and all the juice from the cinnamon apple rings. Next morning, remove ducks from marinade and coat with flour and brown in hot oil or butter (brown all over). Prepare stuffing mix per directions on package and add celery, onions, apples, and water chestnuts to dressing mix. Stuff ducks with dressing. Place ducks in covered roaster and pour more wine and the marinade juice over the ducks and then smother with the orange marmalade. Cover and bake 3 hours or until tender at 325°.

Grace Berg

Pheasant Supreme

Pheasant at our house is cooked like chicken, though we may add sauce such as this pheasant supreme.

Easy
Serves: 3 to 4

Preparation Time: 30 minutes
Cooking Time: 1 ½ hours

1 pheasant
1 pint sour cream
½ cup sherry
2 stalks celery, diced
1 small onion, chopped

½ apple, diced
1 small carrot, diced
flour seasoned with salt
  and pepper

Cut up pheasant as you would a chicken to fry. Roll each piece in seasoned flour. Brown pieces in Dutch oven in oil. Pour off excess fat and add sour cream, sherry, celery, onion, apple, and carrots to the browned pheasant. Allow to simmer for one hour or until the bird is tender. Remove the pheasant to a warmed platter. Strain liquid and thicken with flour to make gravy. Season with salt and pepper to taste.

Beth McKee

Roast Wild Goose

Here is one recipe that is the simplest and best that I have ever used.

Easy

Serves: 6

Preparation Time: 15 minutes
Baking Time: 2½ to 3 hours
Oven Temperature: 350°

1 wild goose, cleaned thoroughly.
  Be sure to remove all the buckshot!

½ pkg. Lipton dry onion soup mix
1 cup good white wine
1 large "Brown-in-Bag"

Mix onion soup mix with wine. Place goose in the bag and sprinkle with wine and soup mix. Pour extra wine in bag and close. Place in a pan or roaster and bake at 350° for 2½ to 3 hours. Wild goose and wild duck are excellent served with a tart apple-celery salad, cinnamon-flavored baked apples, or orange cups filled with cranberry sauce.

Beth McKee

Baked Wild Duck

May be used for geese also except that the cooking time must be extended depending on the age and toughness of the goose. I have not used this recipe for geese, but it is one of our favorites for cooking a whole duck.

Average

Serves: ½ duck/person

Preparation Time: 1 ½ hours
Cooking Time: 2 hours
Oven Temperature: 300°

1 duck, thoroughly cleaned and
   all the buckshot removed
1 Tbsp. sherry
½ tsp. celery salt
½ tsp. onion salt
½ tsp. celery seed

¼ tsp. curry powder
¼ tsp. pepper
1 tsp. salt
1 small onion, chopped
1 stalk celery, chopped

Place ducks in a pan breast up, sprinkle each with one Tbsp. of sherry. Season each with: ½ tsp. each of celery salt, onion salt and celery seed, ¼ tsp. each of curry and pepper, and 1 tsp. salt. Let seasoned duck set in pan from half to one hour. Chop onion and stalk of celery and place in pan. Bake at 500° until breast is brown (about 20 minutes). Turn and bake until back is brown. Cover and cook one more hour at 300°. If dressing is desired, use any favorite poultry recipe.

Beth McKee

French Ducks

A delicious recipe even for those who do not care for duck. We have sliced the breasts after cooking, and served it in its sauce over crepes for a breakfast following a formal dance. The carcass may be used for soup or hash.

Easy
Serves: 4

Preparation Time: 15 minutes
Cooking Time: 12 to 20 minutes

2 ducks (breasts and legs only)
½ lb. butter
⅔ cup sherry
⅓ cup brandy or whiskey

2 Tbsp. currant jelly
salt and pepper
2 Tbsp. Worcestershire Sauce

Remove breast from two ducks, keeping whole. Put butter in iron skillet, and when melted, add the Worcestershire Sauce, jelly, sherry and brandy or whiskey. Season with salt and pepper. When it boils, put in the duck, turning often with a spoon. Cook 12 to 15 minutes. The legs of the duck are cooked the same except for 5 minutes longer. Very good served over wild rice.

Paul McKee

Wild Sage Chicken Supreme

A perfect dish for the crock pot.

Easy
Serves: 6 to 8

Preparation Time: 15 minutes
Cooking Time: 30 minutes

3 or 4 sage chickens (use only
   breasts and legs)
1 cup chopped onion
1 tsp. salt
½ tsp. pepper

1 Tbsp. parsley
1 Tbsp. poultry seasoning
   (if desired)
1 cup sour cream (optional)
1 can mushroom or celery soup

Lightly flour chickens and brown in oil or butter. Add a small amount of water to browned chicken. Mix onion, salt, seasonings, soup, and sour cream. Add to chicken. The liquid should cover chicken. Cover and cook slowly until tender.

Lila Abercrombie

Smothered Birds

A delicious way to cook any bird.

Average   Preparation Time: 20 minutes
Serves: 4   Cooking Time: 2 hours

birds for 4 people   ½ cup shortening
salt   ¾ cup sauterne or sherry
pepper   3 cups water
garlic powder   1 onion, chopped
lots of paprika   1 can cream of mushroom soup
flour   ¾ cup sour cream
¾ cup mayonnaise   2 Tbsp. parsley

Sprinkle birds with a little garlic powder. Combine flour, salt, pepper and paprika in plastic bag. Shake birds in mixture. Brown in Dutch oven in hot shortening. Add onion, wine, water and soup. Cover and simmer for two hours. Transfer birds to a platter. Blend sour cream, mayonnaise and parsley with a small amount of the pan juices, then blend this mixture with the remaining pan juices. Pour over birds or serve separately. Good served with rice.

Robin Lightner

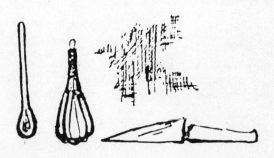

VEGETABLES

VEGETABLES

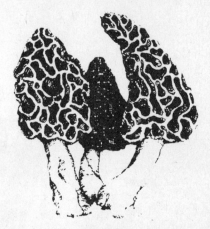

Mushroom Hunting

Winters are long in Jackson Hole. Even the most dedi-
cated skiiers are glad to have the winds turn warm, sending a
receding snow line up the mountains. One of the most pleasur-
able ways to get yourself back outside in the early spring is
mushroom hunting, and two of the choicest mushrooms
abound in this valley. Snow mushrooms can be found while the
snow is still patchy under the pine trees, and a variety of
morel grows along the rivers, coming up about the time the
cottonwoods begin to leaf out. Although these are two of the
easiest mushrooms to identify, the inexperienced mushroomer
should beware. Before eating, be certain of what you've picked!!

Sauteed Mushrooms

Easy
Serves: 6

Preparation Time: 15 minutes
Cooking Time: 15 minutes

1 lb. mushrooms
crushed soda crackers
1 egg

milk
butter

Cut mushrooms to a uniform size, leaving the smaller ones whole. Dip the mushrooms in one egg, beaten and thinned with milk. Roll the mushrooms in the cracker meal and fry in butter until browned.

Judy Montgomery

Mushrooms in Beer Batter

Average
Serves: 6 to 8

Preparation Time: 10 minutes
Refrigerate Batter: 1 hour or more

1 lb. fresh mushrooms
1 can (12 oz.) beer
1 cup flour

1 Tbsp. salt
1 Tbsp. paprika
oil for deep fat frying

With a wire whisk, beat flour, beer, salt and paprika until all lumps are gone, allow batter to rest one hour. Cut mushrooms to a uniform size, leaving the smaller ones whole. Roll the mushrooms in flour, dip in batter and deep fat fry.

Judy Montgomery

Acorn Squash

Easy

Serves: 6

Preparation Time: 10 minutes
Baking Time: 60 to 65 minutes
Oven Temperature: 350°

3 acorn squash
1 small can pineapple tidbits
1 apple, chopped
1 cup chopped celery
¼ cup chopped nuts

½ tsp. salt
½ cup brown sugar
1 tsp. cinnamon
½ cup butter

Cut acorn squash in half and remove seeds. Place cut side down in pan. Bake squash for 45 minutes. Turn squash over. Mix all the other ingredients and fill squash. Return to oven and bake for another 15 to 20 minutes.

Martha Clark

Broccoli, Asparagus, or Green Beans

Very good with wild game.

Easy

Serves: 8

Preparation Time: 20 minutes
Baking Time: 30 minutes
Oven Temperature: 350°

3 pkgs. of frozen vegetables or use fresh if available
2 cans of cream of mushroom soup
¼ cup of vegetable juice (from cooking)

1 small can of water chestnuts
1½ cups of cheese crackers (crushed)
⅔ stick of butter or oleo, melted

Cook vegetables. Lay in a flat casserole. Cup up water chestnuts over top of vegetables. Pour soup mixed with ¼ cup vegetable juice over top. Crush crackers and sprinkle over top. Melt butter and dribble over top. Bake at 350° for ½ hour, uncovered.

Beth McKee

Chopped Broccoli Casserole

Average

Yield: 2 quart casserole

Preparation Time: 30 minutes
Cooking Time: 1 hour
Oven Temperature: 350°

2 pkgs. of chopped frozen broccoli
½ cup Miracle Whip
½ cup commercial bread crumbs

1 can cream of mushroom soup
1 cup diced strong cheese

Cook broccoli according to package instructions, mix in salad dressing, soup, and cheese. Prepare the night before using and let stand in refrigerator. Sprinkle with bread crumbs just before baking. Bake in two quart baking dish.

Carol Yearsley

Rice & Broccoli Casserole

Easy

Serves: 6

Preparation Time: 20 minutes
Baking Time: 20 minutes
Oven Temperature: 400°

2 Tbsp. finely chopped celery
2 Tbsp. finely chopped onion
2 Tbsp. butter
1 small jar Cheez Whiz
1 can mushroom soup
1½ cups cooked rice

1 pkg. chopped broccoli, cooked
   and drained
salt to taste
a little white pepper
¼ cup slivered almonds

Saute celery and onions; stir in cheese, soup, broccoli, rice, salt, dash of pepper and nuts. Bake at 400° for 20 minutes. Serves 6. Good with chicken, baked or fried.

Jane Skeoch

Golden Corn and Mushroom Bake

Similar to a souffle.

Easy

Serves: 4

Preparation Time: 10 minutes
Baking Time: 40 minutes
Oven Temperature: 350°

1 12-oz. can whole kernel corn
2 eggs, beaten
1 4-oz. can button mushrooms
½ tsp. salt

¼ tsp. onion salt
½ cup cracker crumbs
2 Tbsp. butter
½ cup milk

Add drained corn to beaten eggs and pour into 1½ quart buttered baking dish. Drain mushrooms, reserving ¼ cup of the liquid. Stir mushrooms and salts into corn mixture. Sprinkle with cracker crumbs and dot with butter. Add reserved mushroom liquid to milk and pour over crumbs. Bake uncovered.

Sue Everett

Mexican Cream Corn

Easy   *Preparation Time: 20 minutes*
Serves: 4   *Cooking Time: 30 minutes*

2 pkgs. frozen corn   4 green chilies
4 Tbsp. butter   ½ tsp. salt
1 onion, chopped   ¾ cup Swiss cheese
1 clove garlic, crushed   sour cream

Saute onions and garlic in butter. Add thawed corn, green chilies chopped, salt and cheese cubed. Cover with a towel and cook over low heat stirring occasionally for about 30 minutes. Serve with a bowl of sour cream.

Cookbook Committee

Stuffed Mushrooms

Marvelous for a light luncheon and oh, so low calorie!

Easy   *Preparation Time: 20 minutes*
Serves: 3 to 4

12 extra large mushrooms   1 small can crab
1 Tbsp. butter   6 Tbsp. cottage cheese
¼ cup chopped onion   salt and pepper
3 Tbsp. bread crumbs

Wash mushrooms thoroughly and remove stems. Chop stems. In large frying pan slowly saute mushroom caps in the butter until almost tender. Remove from pan and keep warm. Saute onion and mushroom stems. When tender, add crab, bread crumbs, and cottage cheese. Season with salt and pepper. When just heated through, pile into mushroom caps and serve. This is also very good without the crab.

Marge D'Atri

Onion Tart

Average

Yield: One 9-inch pie

Preparation Time: 30 minutes
Baking Time: 30 minutes
Oven Temperature: 350°

1½ cup Ritz Cracker crumbs
10 Tbsp. butter
4 cups onions, sliced thinly
4 Tbsp. flour
1 cup hot milk

½ cup hot chicken stock
½ cup sour cream
1 egg yolk, beaten
1 cup grated Longhorn Cheese

Mix cracker crumbs with 4 Tbsp. butter and press into 9" pie pan. Saute onions in 2 Tbsp. butter. Set aside. Melt remaining butter in pan, stir in flour mixing well. Add milk and chicken stock and stir until thickened. Add sour cream mixed with egg yolk. Add onions and season to taste. Pour into crust. Sprinkle cheese on top and bake at 350° for 25 to 30 minutes.

Robin Lightner

Potato Pancakes

Average
Serves: 4

Preparation Time: 30 minutes

1 cup mashed potatoes, leftovers
    or instant
1 green onion, minced
1 Tbsp. baking powder
½ cup flour

¼ cup milk or cream
½ cup grated Cheddar cheese
1 egg
salt and pepper to taste

Beat egg, add onion, baking powder, milk, cheese, and salt and pepper. Mix well, add to potatoes. Melt butter in skillet. Drop potato mixture by spoonfuls as you would do pancakes. Brown on both sides. Serve hot.

Robin Lightner

Zucchini Quiche

Great for a brunch!!
Complicated

Preparation Time: 30 minutes
Cooking Time: 30 minutes
Oven Temperature: 350°

Serves: 6 to 8

1 lb. of zucchini, peeled and
  coarsely grated
2 tsp. of salt
4 egg yolks, beaten
1 medium onion, grated
½ cup Parmesan cheese, fresh
  and grated

1 large potato, boiled, peeled
  and mashed
1 Tbsp. olive oil
1 clove garlic, crushed
salt and pepper to taste
4 egg whites, beaten

After peeling and grating zucchini, sprinkle with two teaspoons of salt and let stand for ten minutes. Put zucchini, a portion at a time, in a piece of cheesecloth and squeeze out all moisture. In a bowl, combine zucchini with egg yolks, onion, cheese, potato, oil, and garlic. Add salt and pepper to taste. Beat egg whites with a pinch of salt until they hold very stiff peaks. Fold whites into zucchini mixture. Pour into a lightly oiled 9-inch pie pan. Sprinkle with ⅓ cup of Parmesan cheese and lay five strips of bacon across the top. Bake at 350° for 30 minutes or until well browned.

Cookbook Committee

Potato and Nut Croquettes

Average
Yield: 12 croquettes

Preparation Time: 45 minutes

2 cups hot, riced potatoes
4 cups milk
1 tsp. salt
½ tsp. pepper
¼ tsp. cayenne

½ cup pecan nuts, chopped
bread crumbs
1 egg yolk
1 tsp. cold water

Mix potatoes, milk, salt, peppers, and nuts with fork until light. Shape into small croquettes and roll in bread crumbs. Dip in egg which has been mixed with cold water. Roll in bread crumbs again, and fry until golden brown in deep fat. Drip on unglazed paper and serve. (Makes approximately 12 croquettes.)

Rosemary Laumeyer

Vegetable Lasagne

Average

Serves: 8 to 10

Preparation Time: 45 minutes
Baking Time: 30 minutes
Oven Temperature: 375°

10 lasagne noodles
1 lb. fresh spinach
2 cups (5 oz.) fresh mushrooms
1 cup grated carrots
½ cup chopped onion
1 Tbsp. oil
1 15-oz. can tomato sauce

1 6-oz. can tomato paste
½ cup chopped, pitted, ripe olives
1½ tsp. oregano
2 cups cottage cheese, drained
16-oz. mozzarella cheese
grated Parmesan cheese

Cook noodles in boiling water until tender, then drain. Rinse spinach well and cook in covered pan without additional water. Reduce heat when steam forms and cook for 3 to 5 minutes. Cook mushrooms, carrots and onion in oil until they are tender, but not brown. To this mixture add tomato sauce, tomato paste, olives and oregano. Layer ½ each of noodles, cottage cheese, spinach, mozzarello and sauce mixture in 13 x 9 x 2" baking dish. Repeat layers. Bake. Let stand 10 minutes before serving.

Jo Case

Mashed Potato Puff

Average

Serves: 6 to 8

Preparation Time: 20 minutes
Baking Time: 45 minutes
Oven Temperature: 350°

4 cups hot mashed potatoes
   (may be instant)
¼ cup butter
½ cup milk, or more if needed
8 oz. softened cream cheese

1 egg
¼ cup chopped pimento
¼ cup finely chopped onion
paprika

Grease 2 quart baking dish. Prepare potatoes with butter and milk; mix in cream cheese. Beat in egg, pimento, and onion. Turn into baking dish. Dot with butter, sprinkle with paprika. Cover, and bake at 350⁰ for 45 minutes.

Alice Glass

Ratatouille

A good blend of flavors.

Average   *Preparation Time: 20 minutes*
                                             Baking Time: 1 hour and 20 minutes
Serves: 6 to 8   *Oven Temperature: 350°*

¾ lb. summer squash   1 large onion
2¼ tsp. salt   2 bell peppers
3 large cloves of garlic   ½ tsp. marjoram
6 Tbsp. oil   3 Tbsp. red wine
1 tsp. cumin seed   3 tomatoes
1 small eggplant   1 tsp. dill weed
1 tsp. oregano

Slice squash into large (3 qt.) casserole with lid. Sprinkle with ¾ tsp. salt, 1 clove minced garlic, 2 Tbsp. oil and the cumin seed, crushed. Peel eggplant, slice and arrange over squash. Sprinkle with ¾ tsp. salt, 1 clove garlic, minced, 2 Tbsp. oil and the oregano. Thinly slice onion, spread over eggplant, top with sliced green peppers. Sprinkle with remaining salt, garlic, oil, marjoram, and the wine. Cover and bake 1 hour. Arrange sliced tomatoes over the peppers, sprinkle with dill and bake uncovered for an additional 20 minutes.

Judy Montgomery

Indian Rice

Average   *Preparation Time: 45 minutes*
Serves: 6

1⅓ cups regular rice   2 Tbsp. butter
¼ cup finely sliced onion   ¼ cup dark raisins

Prepare rice according to your method. Saute onions in butter, until limp, and then add raisins and heat thoroughly. Mix onions, raisins, and rice in a covered dish. Serves six.

Jane Skeoch

Sweet Potato Souffle

A delicious accompaniment for a roast turkey.

Average   *Preparation Time: 30 minutes*
                                       Baking Time: 55 minutes
Serves: 10   *Oven Temperature: 400° and 350°*

3 cups mashed, cooked, sweet   1 cup white sugar
   potatoes   1 tsp. salt
1 cup crushed pineapple   1 tsp. vanilla
3 eggs, separated, beat whites   ½ stick butter
   stiff   ¼ tsp. ginger
½ cup Carnation canned milk   ¼ tsp. nutmeg
1 tsp. cinnamon

Beat mixture until smooth and fluffy. Fold in stiffly beaten egg whites. Pour into a buttered souffle dish.

TOPPING:
1 cup brown sugar   1 cup pecans, chopped
½ cup flour

Mix and sprinkle over sweet potato mixture. Cook in a pre-heated 400⁰ oven for 10 minutes. Lower temperature to 350⁰ and continue baking for approximately 45 more minutes.

Alice Glass

Zucchini Casserole

Average   *Preparation Time: 20 minutes*
                                        Cooking Time: ½ hour
Serves: 4   *Oven Temperature: 350°*

4 cups zucchini   1 chopped onion
3 eggs   1 chopped green pepper
1 cup Parmesan cheese   dash of salt and pepper
¾ cup mayonnaise   1 cup bread crumbs
¼ cup sour cream   butter, 1/8 cup or less

Boil zucchini to get water out of it; for less than five minutes. Grease casserole, add zucchini. Mix all the other ingredients together and pour over zucchini. Mix well. Dot the top with butter and sprinkle with bread crumbs. Bake at 350⁰ for 30 minutes.

Kathy Phillips

Spinach Quiche

This can be done with frozen spinach and without a pastry shell.

Average

Serves: 6 as main course

Preparation Time: 15 minutes
Baking Time: 25 to 30 minutes
Oven Temperature: 375°

1 9" unbaked pie shell
2 lbs. fresh spinach
2 Tbsp. chopped onion
2 Tbsp. butter
3 eggs, beaten

1½ cups heavy cream
¼ cup grated Gruyere cheese
½ tsp. nutmeg
salt and pepper to taste

Wash spinach and discard thick stems. Blanche spinach in boiling water for 1 minute, drain and pat dry with paper towels. Chop spinach and onions finely and cook in butter until all liquid has evaporated. Combine eggs, cream, salt, pepper, and nutmeg, add to spinach mixture and blend well. Pour into a 9" pie pan lined with flaky pie crust, sprinkle with cheese and dot with butter.

Robin Lightner

Spinach-Rice Ring

Average
Serves: 8 to 10

Preparation Time: 45 minutes

2 cups of rice
6 cups of water
2 tsp. of salt

3 pkgs. of frozen spinach
3 cans of baby beets (16 to 17 oz.)
garlic salt

Cook rice in boiling salted water until very soft. Drain but leave enough water so rice is moist. Cook spinach according to the package directions, add small sprinkle of garlic salt, after spinach is broken up. Drain and combine spinach and rice and press into a heated 2½ quart ring mold. Turn out on a hot platter. Fill center with beets which have been heated, seasoned and sauced with butter.

Josephine C. Fabian

Jane's Sweet Potatoes

Easy

Serves: 8

Preparation Time: 1 hour
Baking Time: 1 hour
Oven Temperature: 350°

6 medium sweet potatoes
1 cup brown sugar
½ cup white sugar
2 Tbsp. cornstarch

dash of salt
¾ to 1 cup orange juice
¾ to 1 cup water
4 Tbsp. butter

Peel and slice potatoes and cook covered with water and dash of salt until just tender; drain and arrange in shallow buttered casserole. Pour sauce over and bake at 350° for one hour.
SAUCE:
Mix sugars, cornstarch and salt. Add orange juice and water slowly and cook until clear and slightly thickened. Add butter.

Jane Skeoch

Quick Potato Bake

Average

Serves: 8 to 10

Preparation Time: 1½ hours
Baking Time: 30 minutes
Oven Temperature: 350°

1 dozen new potatoes
1 cup grated American cheese
1 can cream of celery soup or
    mushroom soup
½ cup milk

1 Tbsp. parsley
½ cup grated cheese
salt and pepper

Boil potatoes until done. Slice the potatoes very thin. Place in a 2 quart casserole or a 13 x 9" pan. Alternate layers of potatoes, grated cheese, and soup mixed with milk. Season with salt and pepper. Garnish top with more grated cheese and sprinkle with parsley. Bake in a 350° oven for 30 minutes.

Jane Hurst

Spinach with Artichokes

Easy

Serves: 4

Preparation Time: 15 minutes
Baking Time: 25 minutes
Oven Temperature: 350°

1 pkg. frozen chopped spinach
1 3-oz. pkg. cream cheese
salt
pepper
cracker crumbs

1 can artichoke hearts—bottoms
    are better, but very expensive
2 Tbsp. butter
sliced water chestnuts, optional

Cook spinach according to package directions. Drain, squeezing out excess water. Return to stove. Add butter, cream cheese, salt and pepper and chestnuts. Butter a small casserole dish, spread bottom with chopped artichokes. Spread spinach mixture on top of artichokes. Sprinkle cracker crumbs on top.

Cookbook Committee

Broiled Tomatoes

A favorite of ours for cook-outs.

Easy

Serves: 6

Preparation Time: 20 minutes
Baking Time: 20 to 30 minutes
Oven Temperature: 400°

6 large tomatoes or 12 small ones
¾ cup minced onion
¼ tsp. curry powder
¼ tsp. sugar (or more)

¼ cup butter
2 Tbsp. chopped parsley
½ tsp. salt

Cut the large tomatoes in half or cut a slice off the top of each small one. Melt the butter and mix it with the remaining ingredients. Put a spoonful of the mixture on top of each tomato. These may be broiled (be sure they get hot through), baked in a flat dish in a 400° oven for 20 to 30 minutes depending on size of tomatoes, or wrapped in foil and cooked on your campfire grill.

Mary Mead

Northern Grits

Try these for brunch!

Easy

Serves: 6 to 8

Preparation Time: 10 minutes
Baking Time: 1 hour
Oven Temperature: 350°

1 cup grits
4 cups water
1 tsp. salt
½ cup margarine

1 roll Kraft garlic cheese
3 eggs, plus enough milk to make
    1 cup liquid

Bring water to boil, add the grits and salt and boil for 3 minutes. Stir in remaining ingredients and turn into buttered casserole. Bake for one hour at 350⁰.

Dottie Larentzen
Sandy Bommer

Jewish Noodles

Cut recipe in half if you do not need so much.

Easy

Serves: 12

Preparation Time: 10 minutes
Cooking Time: 30 minutes
Oven Temperature: 350°

2 pkgs. Lipton chicken noodle
    soup mix -OR- onion soup mix
6 cups water

1 16-oz. pkg. vermicelli noodles
3 pints of sour cream

Bring soup mix and water to a boil and add vermicelli. Boil for ten minutes. Grease a casserole dish well. Add sour cream to the soup mix, water and vermicelli. Bake uncovered in a 350⁰ oven for 30 minutes.

Marsha Holden

Spoon Bread Souffle

The kids love this, but it is nice enough to serve to company.

Average

Serves: 6

Preparation Time: 30 minutes
Baking Time: 50 minutes
Oven Temperature: 350°

2 cups milk
½ cup corn meal
¼ lb. butter
5 oz. Kraft garlic-flavored cheese,
   or milk cheese, shredded, and
1 clove garlic, crushed

4 eggs, separated
1 tsp. baking powder
1 tsp. salt
1 tsp. sugar

Combine milk and corn meal in a saucepan. Cook and stir over medium heat until mixture attains the consistency of thick cream sauce. Take care not to burn it. Remove from heat and add the butter, stirring so it melts. Add garlic cheese and stir until smooth. Cool. Beat egg yolks with corn meal mixture, adding baking powder, salt, and sugar. Mix well. Beat egg whites to stiff peaks and fold in. Pour in a well-buttered two quart souffle dish. Bake in a pre-heated 350° oven for 45 to 50 minutes, until top is puffed and golden.

Alice Glass

Wild Rice Casserole

Excellent with wild game.

Easy

Serves: 6

Preparation Time: 30 minutes
Cooking Time: 30 minutes
Oven Temperature: 325°

1 cup wild rice
1 large onion, chopped fine
1 medium-sized can mushrooms
salt to taste

1 Tbsp. butter or margarine
2 cups thick white sauce -OR-
   2 cans of mushroom soup

Boil rice in salted water until done. Do not overcook. Saute onion, chopped fine in butter. Do not brown. Add mushrooms. Make two cups medium thick white sauce or use two cans of mushroom soup undiluted. Add all ingredients, pour into buttered casserole. Bake at 325 degrees until thoroughly heated through. About thirty minutes. To make wild rice go further: You may use half wild rice and half white rice.

Fran Mosley

Joanne Hennes

SWEETS

DESSERTS

Almond Custard Meringue Alla Ricca

Very complicated

Serves: 10

Preparation Time: 15 minutes
Baking Time: 1½ hours
Chilling Time: 2 hours

5 egg whites at room temp.
pinch of salt
¾ cup plus 1 Tbsp. sugar
½ tsp. almond extract
¾ cup sliced toasted almonds

2 Tbsp. softened butter
2 cups custard (next step)
1 cup whipped cream flavored
  with 2 Tbsp. sugar

Beat egg whites with salt. When foamy, add sugar until it stands in soft peaks. Liberally grease a 9-inch ring mold with butter. Sprinkle bottom and sides with ½ cup of the toasted almonds. Carefully spoon in meringue. Place mold in shallow pan filled with hot water. Bake in 250 degree oven. Bake 1½ hours or until puffed and springs back when pressed. Remove from oven. Let stand 10 minutes. Reverse mold on large plate. Give sharp tap with wooden spoon on mold and lift off. Let cool and then refrigerate two hours. Fill center with custard and decorate.

CUSTARD:

2½ cups light cream
1½ tsp. vanilla
8 egg yolks

pinch of salt
¾ cup sugar
½ to 1 package gelatin

Soften gelatin in a little water. Place cream in heavy saucepan. Stir in gelatin and simmer for about 10 minutes. Meanwhile, beat yolks with salt and sugar until well mixed. Slowly stir hot cream into egg mixture. Use a double boiler or cook egg/cream mixture over low heat until it thickens and coats the back of a spoon. (It should be the consistency of a cream pie filling.) Add vanilla. Cool, then cover with wax paper to prevent a crust from forming. Refrigerate until it begins to set like jello. Then assemble.

To assemble: spoon custard in center of meringue. Top with remaining almonds. Cover center (custard) with whipped cream and pipe swags of whipped cream in three lines around the sides of meringue. Decorate top with chocolate leaves or chocolate cornacopias.

Robin Lightner

Chocolate Leaves

Pick medium-size firm leaves from garden. Wash and dry. Melt semi-sweet chocolate on stove and spread back of leaf with chocolate. Freeze. When set, gently pull off leaf and keep in freezer until ready to use.

Note: Leaves must be firm or they will not peel. Also your hands are 98 degrees and if you handle leaves too long, you will melt the chocolate.

Robin Lightner

Chocolate Cornucopias

Melt a few squares of semi-sweet chocolate in small double boiler. Remove from heat and blend. Have ready cornu- copias made from wax paper. To make, cut wax paper in 4 to 5 inch squares. Cut each square into a triangle. Form a cone from triangle. Secure with tape so it won't unroll. With small pointed paring knife, spread inside of cone with chocolate. Place in freezer a few minutes until set and firm. Gently peel off wax paper. Return to freezer until ready to use.

Robin Lightner

Banana Chill Dessert

Easy
Serves: 15

Preparation Time: 25 minutes
Chilling Time: 1 hour

2 cups graham crackers
2 sticks margarine, softened
2 eggs
2 cups powdered sugar
1 large can crushed pineapple

2 bananas, sliced
1 large carton of Cool Whip
1 pkg. of Dream Whip
1 small pkg. of pecans, chopped
¼ cup cherries, chopped

Crush graham crackers and mix with one stick of margarine. Press into 9 x 13" pan and bake at 350° for five minutes. Cool while making filling. Beat together eggs, powdered sugar and the last stick of margarine. Spread over crust. Drain pineapple, reserving juice. Slice bananas and soak in pineapple juice for a few minutes. Arrange banana slices on top of egg mixture. Then spread pineapple on top of bananas. Spread Cool Whip on top and chill. Meanwhile, whip Dream Whip. Fold nuts and cherries into Dream Whip. Spread on top before serving.

Jeanne Houfek

Blueberry Dessert

Average

Serves: 12 to 15

Preparation Time: 50 minutes
Baking Time: 20 minutes
Cooking Time: 15 minutes
Oven Temperature: 375°

20 graham crackers
¼ lb. butter
3 cups sugar
2 eggs

1 8-oz. cream cheese
1 tsp. vanilla
3½ Tbsp. cornstarch
1 pkg. blueberries (1 lb.)

Mix crumbs, butter, and ½ cup sugar. Lightly pack in 9 x 13" pan. Beat eggs, cream cheese, 1½ cups sugar and vanilla until fluffy. Add to crumb mixture. Bake 20 minutes at 375°. Cool. Cook berries, cornstarch and remaining sugar until thick. Cool, spread evenly over crust. Chill, top with whipped cream if desired.

Jennifer Clark

Charlie's Orange Souffle

Average
Serves: 8

Preparation Time: Stage I   20 minutes
Stage II 10 minutes
Baking Time: 30 minutes

STAGE I
½ cup flour
⅓ cup butter
¾ cup milk, boiling hot
¼ cup orange juice
1 tsp. grated orange rind
7 egg yolks

STAGE II
6 egg whites
⅓ cup sugar

Knead flour and butter together until it is thoroughly combined, then work it into the boiling milk and add orange juice. Do not cook it; just work together over low heat to make a stiff paste. Add orange rind and egg yolks and mix well. Beat egg whites, adding sugar gradually after they have formed soft peaks, and continue beating until they are stiff but not dry. Fold them into first mixture. Pour into a well-buttered and sugared 8-cup souffle mold and bake on bottom shelf at 450⁰ for 10 minutes, then reduce the heat to 375⁰ and continue cooking about 20 minutes longer, until puffed and golden brown. Must serve as soon as it comes from the oven! Serve with Rich Vanilla Sauce. (page 138)

TO MAKE AHEAD: Prepare through Stage I. When main course is served, add Stage II and put in oven. Serve immediately from oven!

Rich Vanilla Sauce

Yields: 2½ cups   *Cooking Time: 20 minutes*

4 egg yolks
½ cup sugar
pinch of salt

2 cups light cream, scalding hot
1 tsp. vanilla extract or Grand
Marnier or Cointreau

Beat together yolks, sugar, and salt and pour hot cream slowly into mixture while heating briskly. Cook over very low heat or in top of a double boiler, stirring constantly with a wooden spoon, until sauce thickens enough to coat the back of a spoon. Remove quickly from the heat and set into pan of cold water. Add vanilla and stir until it cools. Serve cold.

Robin Lightner

Chocolate Icebox Dessert

Really rich!!!

Average   *Preparation Time: 20 minutes*
Serves: 9

2 cups powdered sugar
2 Tbsp. cocoa
¼ tsp. salt
½ cup butter

2 eggs
½ cup nuts
1 tsp. vanilla
1 cup vanilla wafer crumbs

Sift sugar, cocoa and salt together. Cream butter and sugar mixture. Add unbeaten yolks, one at a time. Beat well and add nuts and flavoring. Fold in egg whites which have been beaten until stiff. Spread the vanilla wafer crumbs in a 9 x 9" pan, spread mixture on top. Top with a dabble of whipped cream. Instead of using wafer crumbs, you may put the filling in a baked pie shell.

Jennifer Clark
Sue Everett

English Plum Pudding

Complicated   *Preparation Time: 40 minutes*
Serves: 16   *Cooking Time: 4 hours*

1 cup flour
1 tsp. soda
1 tsp. salt
1 tsp. cinnamon
⅔ tsp. mace
¼ tsp. nutmeg
1½ cup cut up raisins (½ lb.)
2 cups currants (½ lb.)
¼ cup fruit juice

¾ cup finely cut up citron (¼ lb.)
⅓ cup each cut up candied
   orange and lemon peel
½ cup finely chopped walnuts
1½ cups soft bread crumbs
2 cups ground suet (½ lb.)
1 cup brown sugar, packed
3 eggs, beaten
⅓ cup currant jelly

Grease well a two quart ring mold. Put flour, soda, salt, cinnamon, mace and nutmeg into a large bowl. Stir in fruits, nuts, and bread crumbs. Combine suet, brown sugar, eggs, jelly and fruit juice. Mix into flour-fruit mixture. Pour into mold. Cover with foil. (You may freeze it at this point, if you wish.)

Place rack in large pot and pour boiling water into pan, up to level of rack. Put mold on rack. Cover pot. Keep water boiling over low heat and steam pudding four hours, or until wooden pick inserted in center comes out clean. Keep an eye on level of water in steaming pot. Unmold. Cut into slices and serve warm with Hard Sauce.

HARD SAUCE:
½ cup butter or margarine,
   softened

1 cup confectioners sugar
2 tsp. vanilla

Mix all ingredients. Chill.

Anne E. Kaunitz

Mint Delight

A good "make ahead" recipe. Nice at Christmas time.

Average
Serves: 12 to 15

Preparation Time: 30 minutes
Freeze: 6 hours or more

CRUST:
2 cups vanilla wafer crumbs
½ cup melted butter

FILLING:
½ cup melted butter
1½ cup powdered sugar
3 eggs, beaten
3 squares unsweetened chocolate
1½ cups cream, whipped
1 pkg. miniature marshmallows
½ cup crushed peppermint candy

Make crumb crust out of vanilla wafer crumbs and butter. Cream ½ cup butter and sugar, add eggs and melted chocolate. Beat until light and fluffy; spoon over crumb crust; set in freezer. Whip cream, fold in marshmallows, spread over chocolate layer, sprinkle candy over top—put in freezer. Freeze 6 hours or more.

Carol McCain

Peach Freeze

Easy

Serves: 4

Preparation Time: 15 minutes
Refrigeration Time: 1 hour
Freezer Time: 1 hour or more

4 peaches, diced
1¼ cups sour cream
½ cup sugar

1 tsp. lemon juice
¼ tsp. almond extract

Put into blender and blend until smooth. Pour into 9" square metal pan and place in freezer for approximately 1 hour, until solid, but not hard. Put into large mixing bowl and beat at medium speed until smooth. Pour into molds or individual serving dishes and freeze.

Rosemary Laumeyer

Frosty Strawberry Squares

Easy
Serves: 10 to 13

Preparation Time: 20 minutes
Freezing Time: 6 hours

1 cup sifted flour
¼ cup brown sugar
½ cup chopped walnuts
½ cup butter or margarine, melted
2 egg whites

1 cup granulated sugar
2 cups sliced fresh strawberries*
2 Tbsp. lemon juice
1 cup whipping cream, whipped

(*Or use one 10-oz. pkg. of frozen strawberries, partially thawed; reduce granulated sugar to ⅔ cup.)

Stir together first four ingredients; spread evenly in a shallow baking pan. Bake in 350° oven for 20 minutes, stirring occasionally. Sprinkle ⅔ of the crumbs in a 13 x 9 x 2 inch baking pan. Combine egg whites, sugar, berries, and lemon juice in large bowl; with electric beater, beat at high speed to stiff peaks, about ten minutes. Fold in whipped cream. Spoon over crumbs. Top with remaining crumbs. Freeze six hours or overnight. Cut in 10 to 12 squares. Trim with whole strawberries.

Clare Joy

Fruit Cocktail Dessert

Average

Serves: 10

Preparation Time: 20 minutes
Baking Time: 1 hour
Oven Temperature: 350°

1 can (16-oz.) fruit cocktail
2 eggs, beaten
1 cup sugar
1 cup flour
1 tsp. baking soda

½ tsp. salt

TOPPING:
1 cup brown sugar
½ cup chopped nuts

Mix together all ingredients and put into 10 x 10" ungreased baking pan. Mix together topping ingredients and sprinkle on top of fruit cocktail mixture. Bake at 350° for about an hour or until done in the center. Serve with whipped cream.

Rosemary Laumeyer

Raspberry Dessert

This is a pretty as well as great tasting dessert.

Average   *Preparation Time: 30 minutes*
Serves: 15 to 18   *Chilling Time: 1 to 2 hours*

2 10-oz. pkgs. frozen raspberries   50 marshmallows
1 cup water   1 cup milk
½ cup sugar   2 cups heavy cream, whipped -OR-
2 tsp. lemon juice   2 pkgs. dessert topping mix
4 Tbsp. cornstarch   1¼ cups graham cracker crumbs
¼ cup cold water   ¼ cup nuts, chopped
                                    ¼ cup butter, melted

Heat raspberries with water, sugar, and lemon juice. Dissolve cornstarch in ¼ cup cold water; stir into raspberries and cook until thickened and clear. Cool.

Melt marshmallows in milk over boiling water or in a microwave. Cool thoroughly. Whip cream and fold into marshmallow mixture.

Mix graham cracker crumbs, nuts and butter and press into bottom of a 9 x 13" pan. Spread marshmallow mixture over crumbs. Spread raspberries over marshmallow. Refrigerate until firm.

Any fruit pie filling (canned) may be used for topping instead of raspberry mixture.

Mary Mead

Pumpkin Squares

Outstanding!!!
Average

Yield: 21 squares   *Preparation Time: 20 minutes*
                                   Baking Time: 50 minutes
                                   Oven Temperature: 375°

1 pkg. yellow cake mix   TOPPING:
½ cup melted butter   ¼ cup sugar
1 egg   ½ tsp. cinnamon
FILLING: 2 Tbsp. butter
1 1-lb 14-oz. can Libby's pre-   1 cup cake mix reserved from pkg.
   pared pumpkin pie filling
⅔ cup canned milk
2 eggs

Set aside one cup of cake mix. Mix together the egg, melted butter, and the remaining cake mix. Spread in a greased 9 x 13" cake pan. Mix filling ingredients together and spread over cake mixture. Mix topping ingredients together and sprinkle over pumpkin mixture. Bake in a 375⁰ oven for 50 minutes. Cut into squares and serve with a dollop of whipped cream or Cool Whip.

HIGH ALTITUDE DIRECTIONS:

Add two tablespoons of flour to cake mix before taking out the one cup for topping.

Delores Scarbrough

Sherry Almond Pudding with Sherry Custard Sauce

Easy
Serves: 10 to 12

Preparation Time: 40 minutes
Chilling Time: 4 hours

2 Tbsp. unflavored gelatin
½ cup water, cold
⅓ cup sherry wine
½ tsp. almond extract
¼ tsp. salt
1 cup boiling water

6 egg whites
1½ cups sugar
1 cup almonds, shredded and
   lightly browned
toasted coconut

Soak gelatin in cold water; dissolve in boiling water. Add wine, almond extract and salt. Heat to boiling stirring constantly. Cool. Put in refrigerator. When the mixture begins to thicken, beat until frothy. Beat egg whites until foamy. Gradually add sugar and beat until stiff. Fold the two mixtures together. Chill until almost firm. Pour into a 3-quart melon mold, alternating mixture with one cup of almonds. Chill at least four hours, unmold, garnishing with almond and coconut.

SHERRY CUSTARD SAUCE:

1 pkg. of Dream Whip -OR-
   1 cup whipping cream, whipped
2 cups scalded milk

6 egg yolks
2 Tbsp. flour
¼ cup sugar

Combine all ingredients except whipped cream or Dream Whip. Cook over low heat until thickened, stirring constantly. Cool. When ready to serve, whip one cup of whipping cream and fold into custard. Serve over pudding.

Josephine C. Fabian

Cranberry Pudding

Average

Serves: 6

Preparation Time: 15 minutes
Baking Time: 30 to 35 minutes
Oven Temperature: 350°

3 Tbsp. melted butter
1 cup sugar
2 cups flour
3 tsp. baking powder

¼ tsp. salt
1 cup milk
2 cups whole, raw cranberries

Mix the above ingredients. Bake in a 9 x 9'' pan at 350° for 30 to 35 minutes. Serve warm.

SAUCE:
1 cup sugar
½ cup butter

¾ cup cream

Heat above ingredients to a gradual boil. Serve hot over pudding.

Sandy Bommer

Fruit Fluff

Nice light dessert with a cookie after a heavy meal.

Easy
Serves: 6 to 8

Preparation Time: 30 minutes

1 egg white
1 cup fruit pulp (pureed)
   preferably fresh
½ to 1 cup sugar, depending on
   sweetness of fruit

¼ tsp. cream of tartar
1 tsp. lemon juice, or vanilla,
   or almond extract
1 cup Cool Whip -OR-
   ½ cup whipping cream, whipped

Beat first five ingredients at high speed in mixer for 20 minutes. It will almost triple in bulk. Fold in Cool Whip. Garnish with fresh fruit. Best to eat the day it is made. It does not keep well.

Grace Beardsley

CAKES

Arkansas Cream Cake

Stays moist for a week, you cannot taste the coconut.

Average

Yield: One 8" layer cake

Preparation Time: 30 minutes
Baking Time: 25 to 30 minutes
Oven Temperature: 350°

1 stick butter or margarine
½ cup vegetable shortening
2 cups sugar, less 2 Tbsp.
5 egg yolks
2 cups flour
1 tsp. soda

1 cup buttermilk plus 4 Tbsp.
1 tsp. vanilla
½ cup flake coconut
1 cup chopped pecans
5 egg whites, stiffly beaten

Cream butter and shortening; add sugar and beat until smooth. Add egg yolks and beat well. Combine flour and soda and add to creamed mixture alternately with buttermilk. Stir in vanilla; add coconut and pecans. Fold in beaten egg whites. Pour batter into three well greased and floured 8" cake pans. Bake at 350° for 25 to 30 minutes—or until cake tests done. Cool and frost with following.

FROSTING:

1 8-oz. pkg. of softened cream
  cheese
½ stick of butter

1 box powdered sugar
1 tsp. vanilla
½ cup chopped pecans

Mix cream cheese and butter until smooth. Add sugar and beat well. Add vanilla and chopped pecans. Mix until well blended. Use on COOLED cake.

Should use good pans as this cake is quite heavy and a little hard to handle when removing from pans.

Jane Skeoch

Banana Cake with Chocolate Frosting

This has a very creamy chocolate frosting or without frosting it makes a nice banana bread!!

Average

Yield: One 9" cake

Preparation Time: 20 minutes
Baking Time: 30 minutes
Oven Temperature: 350°

CAKE:

1½ cups sugar
½ cup butter
2 eggs
4 ripe bananas
1 cup whole wheat flour

1¼ cup white flour
¾ tsp. baking soda
½ tsp. baking powder
½ tsp. salt
½ cup sour cream

Cream butter and sugar until light and fluffy. Add eggs, one at a time, incorporating them thoroughly into batter. Add the bananas, beat for one minute. Blend in dry ingredients and sour cream. Beat an additional two minutes. Bake at 350° in 2, greased 9" round cake pans about ½ hour. Remove from pan, cool *completely* before frosting.

FROSTING:

5 squares unsweetened chocolate
4 cups confectioners sugar
6 Tbsp. hot water

2 eggs
⅔ cup butter
1 tsp. vanilla

In medium size mixing bowl, combine sugar, water, butter, eggs, and vanilla. Mix well. Add melted chocolate and blend until just incorporated. Frosting will be very runny at this point. In large size mixing bowl, put a few ice cubes and some cold water, set medium bowl in ice-water, making sure water will not overflow into frosting. Beat until spreading consistency is reached.

Judy Montgomery

Cream Cheese Cupcakes

Excellent!!!

Average   *Preparation Time: 15 minutes*
                                              Baking Time: 40 minutes
Yield: 18 cupcakes   *Oven Temperature: 300°*

CUPCAKES:
3 8-oz. pkgs. of cream cheese, softened
1 cup sugar
5 eggs, at room temperature
1½ tsp. vanilla

TOPPING:
1 cup sour cream
¼ cup sugar
½ tsp. vanilla
cherries

Mix well first four ingredients. Line cupcake pans. Pour in batter until about ¾ full. Bake in a preheated 300° oven for 30 to 40 minutes. Remove from oven. Let stand until topping is ready. Mix sour cream, sugar, and vanilla. Spoon on the top of each cupcake. Trim with cherries. Bake for 5 minutes.

Fran Johnsen

Cheese Filled Lemon Cake

Easy

Serves: 10

Preparation Time: 20 minutes
Cooking Time: 1 hour
Oven Temperature: 350°

1 pkg. yellow cake mix
¼ cup butter -OR- margarine

¾ cup apricot nectar
3 eggs

FILLING:
2 8-oz. pkgs. cream cheese
3 Tbsp. lemon juice

½ cup sugar
1 cup flaked coconut

GLAZE:
2 cups powdered sugar
2 Tbsp. apricot nectar

2 Tbsp. lemon juice

Preheat oven to 350°. Grease and flour 10 inch bundt or tube pan. In a large bowl, combine first four ingredients, beat as directed on cake package. Spoon into prepared pan. In small bowl, combine all Filling ingredients, beat until smooth. Spoon Filling over batter in pan, being careful not to let it touch sides of pan. Bake 50 to 55 minutes, or until top springs back when lightly touched in center. Cool upright in pan for one hour. Remove from pan. Cool. Combine all glaze ingredients until smooth. Drizzle over cake.

HIGH ALTITUDE:
5200 feet, add two tablespoons of flour to cake mix. Bake at 375° for 50 to 55 minutes.

Alice Glass

Different Carrot Cake

Average

Serves: 10 to 12

Preparation Time: 30 minutes
Baking Time: 45 minutes
Oven Temperature: 375°

1 cup oil
2 cups sugar
3 eggs
2 cups flour
2 tsp. soda

1 cup grated or flaked coconut
2 tsp. cinnamon
2 cups grated carrots
1 cup undrained, crushed pine-
　　apple
1 cup nuts

Mix first three ingredients, oil, sugar, and eggs, together. Add remaining ingredients. Mix well. Pour into greased and floured 9 x 13" pan. Bake 45 minutes at 375°. While still warm, glaze with following glaze recipe:

GLAZE:
½ cup buttermilk
1 cup sugar
¾ cup butter

1 tsp. Karo syrup
1 tsp. vanilla

Mix together in saucepan. Bring to boil. Pour over warm cake.

Susie Carlson

Buttermilk Icing

Very fluffy.

Easy
Yield: One sheet cake or a
　　two layer cake

Preparation Time: 15 minutes

½ cup Crisco—not oil
5 Tbsp. buttermilk
1 box powdered sugar

1 tsp. vanilla
1 tsp. butter flavoring

Beat Crisco—add sugar and buttermilk alternately. Spread. You may add cocoa, almond extract, etc., instead of vanilla to change flavor.

Alice Glass

Lady Baltimore Cake

This is a lovely cake, and makes quite a sensation.

Average to Complicated   *Preparation Time: Cake 15 minutes*
                                                        Icing 25 minutes
Serves: 20   *Baking 30 minutes*

CAKE:

1 cup butter   1 cup milk
3 cups sugar   3½ cups cake flour
4 eggs   4 tsp. baking powder
2 tsp. vanilla extract   2 tsp. almond extract
½ cup water

FROSTING:

2 cups sugar   2 tsp. corn syrup
⅔ cup water   2 cups seeded raisins
2 egg whites, beaten stiff   2 cups walnuts
½ cup dates, chopped   ½ cup candied cherries
½ tsp. almond extract   chopped
                                              ½ tsp. vanilla

CAKE:

Use electric mixer and cream butter. Add two cups sugar gradually and heat until consistency of whipped cream. Add eggs and heat thoroughly. Sift baking powder and flour and add alternately with milk to creamed butter and sugar mixture. Bake in three 9" or two 11" greased and floured cake pans in 350° oven 30 minutes. Make a thick syrup of one cup sugar and ½ cup water by bringing to a boil and boiling one minute. Flavor this syrup with almond and vanilla extracts. Spread over cake layers as soon as they are removed from pans.

FROSTING:

Mix sugar, water, syrup. Cook until it forms a firm ball in cold water. Pour gradually into stiffly beaten egg whites, heating constantly. Add raisins, nuts, dates, cherries. Add almond and vanilla extracts. Spread between layers and on top and sides of cake.

Alice Glass

Oatmeal Cake

Average

Yield: One large sheet cake

Preparation Time: 30 minutes
Baking Time: 45 to 60 minutes
Oven Temperature: 350°

List Number 1.

2½ cups boiling water
2 cups quick cook oats
2 sticks margarine

List Number 2.

2 cups sugar
2 cups brown sugar
1 tsp. nutmeg
2 tsp. soda
4 eggs

List Number 3.

2½ cups flour
2 tsp. cinnamon
2 tsp. salt

Mix ingredients in List Number 1. Cover and let stand 20 minutes. Then add ingredients in List Number 2. Mix well. Add ingredients in List Number 3. Pour into greased and floured 9" x 13" pan. Bake 45 to 60 minutes (until center springs back when touched) at 350°. Frost.

ICING:

2 cups coconut
2 tsp. vanilla
1 cup sugar

½ cup milk
1 stick soft margarine
2 cups nuts

Combine and bring to a boil. Pour over warm cake. Brown under broiler -OR- frost with Cream Cheese Icing or Buttermilk Icing. (page 149)

Alice Glass
Sandy Bommer

Pineapple-Nut Cake

Average

Yield: One 9 x 13" cake

Preparation Time: 15 minutes
Baking Time: 60 to 70 minutes
Oven Temperature: 350°

1 can Thank-You brand pineapple
   pie filling
2 cups flour
1 cup sugar
1½ tsp. soda

1 tsp. salt
2 eggs, beaten
1 tsp. vanilla
⅔ cup Crisco oil
¾ cup chopped nuts, if desired

Mix all ingredients in 9" x 13" pan—do not grease pan. Bake at 350° for one hour.

GLAZE:
½ tsp. vanilla
1 cup powdered sugar

2 Tbsp. milk

Combine ingredients. Pour over cake while hot.

Barbara VanGenderen

Sand Cake
(The Swedish name is Sandkaka)

This is an amazingly good dessert!!

Average

Serves: 10 to 12

Preparation Time: 45 minutes
Baking Time: 1 hour
Oven Temperature: 300°

1 cup butter, scant
¾ cup flour
2 tsp. baking powder
1 cup sugar, scant

¾ cup potato flour
3 eggs
2 Tbsp. brandy
bread crumbs

Melt butter and cool. Sift together flour and baking powder. Work butter, sugar, and potato flour until white and fluffy. Add eggs and continue to beat. Add brandy and flour, stir until well blended and pour into a well buttered and bread-crumbed deep round cake pan. Bake in slow oven (300°) for one hour.

Freida B. Chase

Rum Cake

This has always been a winner.

Easy

Preparation Time: 10 minutes
Baking Time: 1 hour

Yield: One 10" tube cake pan

Oven Temperature: 350°

1 pkg. yellow cake mix
1 small pkg. instant vanilla
  pudding
4 eggs
½ cup cold water

½ cup Wesson Oil
½ cup Bacardi dark rum
1 cup chopped pecans

Set oven at 350°. Grease and flour 10" tube pan. Sprinkle nuts over bottom of pan. Mix all cake ingredients together and beat 2 minutes with electric mixer. Pour batter over nuts and bake 1 hour. Cool. Invert on serving plate. Poke cake with fork so holes go all the way to the bottom, all over cake. Dribble glaze* over top. All cake to absorb glaze—keep repeating until used up. Keep in covered cake plate until ready to serve. Serve with whipped cream or ice cream.

GLAZE*

¼ lb. butter or margarine
1 cup granulated sugar

¼ cup water
½ cup Bacardi Rum

Melt butter in saucepan. Stir in water, sugar and boil five minutes, stirring constantly. Remove from heat and stir in rum.

Anne E. Kaunitz

Sherry-Poppy Seed Cake

Very different flavor and everyone seems to like it. May be served unfrosted—it's just as good!

Easy

Yield: One 10" tube cake

Preparation Time: 10 minutes
Baking Time: 45 minutes
Oven Temperature: 350°

1 box yellow cake mix
1 pkg. instant vanilla pudding
4 eggs
½ cup cream sherry

1 cup sour cream
⅓ cup poppy seeds
½ cup butter-flavored oil

Mix all ingredients. Beat 2 minutes at high speed. Bake in greased and floured tube or bundt pan, or in 2 layer pans. Bake 45 minutes at 350° in bundt or tube pans—bake only 30 minutes in layer pans. Frost with Sherry Flavored Creamed Cheese Icing, or White Butter Icing.

Yvonne Pfaff

Surprise Applesauce Cake

This cake is "cheese-cake" like.

Easy
Serves: 8
Yield: 10" deep cake pan or
springform pan

Preparation Time: 20 minutes
Cooking Time: 50 to 60 minutes
Oven Temperature: 350°

2 Tbsp. butter, melted
½ tsp. cinnamon
2 cups graham cracker crumbs
3 eggs, separated

1⅓ cups (1 can) Eagle Brand
    Sweetened Condensed Milk
2 Tbsp. lemon juice
grated rind of one lemon
2 cups of applesauce

Add butter and cinnamon to graham cracker crumbs. Spread thick layer of crumbs on bottom of buttered springform mold or deep 10-inch layer cake pan. Beat egg yolks well, add Eagle Brand Sweetened Condensed Milk, lemon juice, rind and applesauce. Fold in stiffly beaten egg whites. Pour into mold. Cover with remaining cracker crumbs. Bake 50 to 60 minutes at 350°. Serve hot or cold.

Alice Glass

Velvet Almond Fudge Cake

This is like a rich brownie, slice and top with ice cream or cool whip.

Average
Yield: 10" tube cake
One 14 x 10" sheet cake

Preparation Time: 20 minutes
Baking Time: 1 hour, 10 minutes
Oven Temperature: 350°

1½ cups blanched slivered almonds
1 12-oz. pkg. chocolate chips
1 2-layer size pkg. chocolate fudge or chocolate cake mix
1 4-serving size pkg. Jell-o chocolate fudge or chocolate flavor instant pudding and pie filling

4 eggs
1 cup sour cream
½ cup water
¼ cup oil
½ tsp. each vanilla and almond extract

Chop almonds and toast at 350° for 3 to 5 minutes. Sprinkle ½ cup nuts on bottom of a well greased 10-inch tube pan. Set aside remaining almonds and chocolate chips. Measure remaining ingredients into mixer bowl. Blend and beat four minutes at medium speed. Stir in chips and almonds. Pour into pan. Bake at 350° for one hour and ten minutes, or until cake begins to pull away from sides of pan. DO NOT UNDER-BAKE. Cool in pan 15 minutes. Remove and finish cooling on rack.

Alice Glass

White Fruit Cake

Average

Yield: 4 loaves

Preparation Time: 30 minutes
Baking Time: 3 hours
Oven Temperature: 250°

1 lb. butter
2½ cups sugar
6 eggs
2 oz. lemon extract
1 tsp. soda
3 Tbsp. cooking wine or orange juice

5 cups flour—dredge fruits in 2 cups
1 lb. white raisins
1½ quarts pecans
½ lb. candied red cherries
½ lb. candied pineapple

Cream softened butter and sugar and add egg yolks. Add flour and soda alternately with lemon extract and wine/or orange juice. Add fruits and nuts, which have been dredged in 2 cups of flour. Fold in stiffly beaten egg whites. Place in wax paper lined pans. Bake at 250° for 3 hours. Place a pan of water under cakes while baking.

Jane Skeoch

Fruit Cake

This recipe was baked in large square pans in a wood stove and sold after the Kelly flood. This was one way used to make money to help replace all the belongings lost in the flood!!

Average

Yield: Six 9 x 4" loaves

Preparation Time: 30 minutes
Baking Time: 1 ¾ hours
Oven Temperature: 300°

3 cups sugar
1 lb. butter
8 eggs
1 cup molasses
1 cup sour milk
1 cup strong coffee
1 Tbsp. soda
1 Tbsp. cinnamon

1 Tbsp. allspice or cloves
1 Tbsp. grated nutmeg
½ lb. citron
2 lbs. currants
2 lbs. raisins
1 lb. nuts
9 to 10 cups flour

Mix all ingredients and bake in a moderate oven (300°) for 1¾ hours. Cool loaves before removing from pans.

Ethel Jump

PIES

Cheese Pie

A very smooth and rich dessert.

Easy

Serves: 6

Preparation Time: 15 minutes
Baking Time: 1 hour
Oven Temperature: 350°
Chilling Time: 2 to 3 hours

PIE CRUST:
1⅔ cups graham cracker crumbs
¼ cup sugar
¼ cup soft butter

Blend crust ingredients and pat firmly into a 9-inch pie plate.

FILLING:
12 oz. cream cheese
2 eggs
⅓ cup sugar

Preheat oven to 350°. Beat together the cream cheese, eggs and sugar until smooth. Pour into pie crust. Bake 25 to 30 minutes at 350°. Cool 20 minutes. Raise oven temperature to 375°.

TOPPING:
8 oz. sour cream
2 Tbsp. sugar
1 tsp. vanilla

Cover cooled pie with topping mix and bake 8 minutes at 375°. Chill before serving, about two hours in the refrigerator. Serve as is or top with spoonfuls of sweetened berries.

Marge D'Atri

Buttermilk Pie

Super good, even in a bought pie shell.

Easy
Yield: 8" pie

Preparation Time: 10 minutes
Cooking Time: 1 hour

1 unbaked pie shell—9"
1½ cups sugar
¼ cup flour
dash of salt

½ cup buttermilk
1 tsp. vanilla
3 eggs, beaten
1 stick of butter

Combine all ingredients except butter. Add melted butter. Blend. Pour in an unbaked 9" pie shell. Bake at 350° for one hour.

Hint: Put pecans on bottom of pie shell before adding filling. They will rise to the top.

This is a very Southern pie, but my new Wyoming friends go back for seconds and ask for the recipe.

Robin Lightner

Ella's Flaky Pie Crust

This is a foolproof flaky crust.

Easy

Yield: Three 9" pie crusts

Preparation Time: 10 minutes
Baking Time: 10 minutes
Oven Temperature: 475°

3 cups flour
1¼ cups shortening (Crisco)
dash salt

1 egg
1 Tbsp. vinegar
6 Tbsp. water

Cut shortening into flour and salt. In small bowl or glass, beat remaining ingredients. Combine two mixtures and chill 15 minutes before rolling out. The dough will keep three days in a refrigerator or it may be frozen. For a baked pie crust, prick bottom and bake ten minutes at 475°. Makes three pie crusts.

Robin Lightner

Cheese Topping Apple Pie

Average

Serves: 6

Preparation Time: 40 minutes
Baking Time: 40 minutes
Oven Temperature: 400°

1 9" unbaked pie crust
sour cream
1 cup sugar
1 tsp. ground cinnamon
¼ tsp. ground cloves

6 tart cooking apples
2 Tbsp. flour
1 tsp. grated lemon peel
¼ tsp. salt

TOPPING:
½ cup flour
1/8 tsp. salt
½ stick -OR-
   ¼ cup butter, melted

¼ cup sugar
½ cup grated Cheddar cheese
sour cream

Make flaky pastry substituting sour cream for water. Line 9-inch pie plate with pastry. Prepare apples and slice them thinly. Toss the slices with a mixture of one cup sugar, 2 Tbsp. flour, one teaspoon cinnamon and grated lemon peel, cloves, and salt. Arrange apples overlapping in pan. Combine ½ cup flour with ¼ cup sugar, 1/8 tsp. salt and ½ cup grated cheese. Mix with melted butter. Sprinkle the cheese crumbs over the apples. Bake pie in hot oven (400°) for 40 minutes or until the topping and crust are golden brown. Let pie cool on rack and serve warm, top each slice with a generous spoonful of sour cream.

Jo Case

Fudge Pie

Great dessert to have in the freezer for the drop-in Guests!!

Average

Yield: One 9" pie

Preparation Time: 30 minutes
Baking Time: 20 to 25 minutes
Oven Temperature: 350°

½ cup butter
2 squares unsweetened chocolate
2 eggs

1 cup sugar
¼ cup all-purpose flour
pinch of salt

Melt butter and chocolate over warm water. Beat eggs in a bowl; gradually blend in sugar. Add flour and salt, then combine with chocolate mixture. Pour into ungreased 8" pie plate. Bake at 350° for 20 to 25 minutes. Cool, then freeze. Does not require thawing before serving. Serve with a spoonful of ice cream or whipped cream on top.

Jennifer Clark

Lemon Sponge Cake Pie

This makes an unusual two layer pie. Sponge cake on top, pudding underneath.

Average

Yield: One 8" pie

Preparation Time: 20 minutes
Baking Time: 30 minutes
Oven Temperature: 375°

1 baked pie shell
1 grated lemon rind
1 cup sugar
1 Tbsp. butter
3 egg yolks

2½ Tbsp. flour
1 cup milk
5 Tbsp. lemon juice
3 egg whites

Cream lemon rind, sugar and butter. Beat egg yolks, flour, milk and lemon juice together. Add sugar mixture and beat in. Beat three egg whites until stiff. Fold lightly into custard. Pour into a baked pie shell. Bake in a 375° oven for about 30 minutes.

Marge D'Atri

Puerto Rican Rum Pie

Very fudgy. Right from San Juan.

Average   Preparation Time: Filling - 15 minutes
Serves: 8   Baking - 25 minutes

¼ cup butter   ¼ cup flour
¾ cup brown sugar firmly packed   1 cup coarsely broken walnuts
3 eggs   1 9" pie shell, unbaked
1 12-oz. pkg. semi-sweet choco-   ½ cup walnut halves for
   late pieces, melted   decoration
2 tsp. instant coffee powder   1 tsp. rum extract

Cream butter and sugar. Beat in eggs, one at a time. Add melted chocolate, coffee and rum extract. Add flour and walnut pieces. Place in unbaked pie shell. Top with walnut halves. Bake at 375⁰ for 25 minutes. Top with whipped cream.

Judy Barbour
from her book,
Elegant Elk, Delicious Deer

Pecan Pie

Easy   Preparation Time: 10 minutes
                                   Baking Time: 45 minutes
Serves: 6   Oven Temperature: 325°

1 9" unbaked pie shell   1 cup sugar
1 cup white Karo syrup   3 eggs, beaten
1 tsp. vanilla   1 cup pecans, chopped

Mix all ingredients together. Pour into pie shell. Dot with butter and bake at 325⁰ for 45 minutes. Do not prick pie crust.

Robin Lightner

Mama's Chocolate Pie

Yummy.

Easy
Serves: 8

Cooking Time: 10 minutes

1 baked pie crust
1 cup sugar
4 heaping Tbsp. cocoa
¼ cup and 2 Tbsp. flour

3 eggs
2 cups milk
dash of vanilla

Combine sugar, cocoa and flour in saucepan. Beat eggs, add milk to eggs and then add slowly to sugar mixture. Stir and blend over medium to hot heat. Stir constantly until very thick and bubbly. Add vanilla and pour into baked pie shell. Top with whipped cream flavored with 1 teaspoon of vanilla and 2 teaspoons sugar.

Robin Lightner

San Francisco Apple Pie

This pie takes a bit more time and planning than the usual apple pie, but is absolutely worth the extra effort.

Complicated

Yield: 10 inch pie

Preparation Time: 35 minutes
Baking Time: 40 to 50 minutes
Oven Temperature: 375°

1 10" baked pastry shell
1 stick unsalted butter
6 large, peeled, sliced pippin or
   green apples
¼ cup sugar
¼ cup apricot preserves
1 Tbsp. finely grated lemon rind
2 eggs
½ cup hazelnuts, chopped
   walnuts or pecans

¼ cup dark rum
2 cups sour cream
½ cup packed brown sugar
2 Tbsp. flour
¼ tsp. salt
2 tsp. vanilla
1 tsp. cinnamon
½ cup shredded coconut
2 Tbsp. apricot preserves mixed
   with 1 Tbsp. apricot liqueur

Melt butter in a large skillet. Add the apples and ¼ cup sugar. Stir. Cover and cook over medium-low heat for 10 minutes. Uncover, continue cooking until apples are soft but not falling apart. Stir in the ¼ cup apricot preserves and lemon rind. Cook over brisk heat for 2 minutes. Heat rum in a small pan, ignite, pour flaming rum over apple mixture. Set aside. Preheat oven to 375⁰ F.

Beat together sour cream, brown sugar, flour, salt, vanilla, eggs and cinnamon. Combine half the sour cream mixture with apples. Taste for flavor and correct if sugar or lemon is insufficient.

Paint pastry shell with the 2 Tbsp. apricot preserves mixed with 1 Tbsp. apricot liqueur, and fill with apple mixture. Cover with the remaining sour cream mixture.

Top with coconut and nuts. Bake in upper third of oven until coconut and nuts are toasted. Watch carefully after 15 minutes, but will probably take as long as 30 to 40 minutes. Serve slightly warm.

Alice Glass

Strawberry Chiffon Pie

A husband pleaser.
Average
Serves: 8
1 baked pie shell
1 pkg. gelatin
2 egg yolks
½ cup sugar
1 Tbsp. lemon juice
1 pint whipping cream

Preparation Time: 25 minutes
Chilling Time: 2 hours or longer
½ tsp. almond extract
1 box frozen, sliced strawberries, drained, or 1 carton fresh strawberries sliced, lightly sugared
2 egg whites
fresh strawberries for garnish

Soften gelatin in ¼ cup water. Put beaten egg yolks, gelatin, sugar, and lemon juice in double boiler. Add almond extract. Cook, stirring until it thickens enough to coat the back of a spoon. Add drained strawberries. Whip ½ pint of cream. Whip egg whites. Fold both into cooled strawberry mixture. Add enough red food coloring to tint pink. Pour into baked pie shell and refrigerate several hours. Whip remaining cream with 1 tsp. vanilla and 2 Tbsp. of sugar. Serve each slice with a generous spoon of whipped cream and a fresh strawberry garnish.

Robin Lightner

Raspberry or Strawberry Tart

Average   *Preparation Time: 40 minutes*
Serves: 6

6 individual baked tart shells   1 tsp. vanilla
1 egg, plus one extra yolk   1 tsp. almond extract
1 3-oz. pkg. cream cheese
¼ cup sugar   GLAZE:
3 Tbsp. flour   1 cup red currant jelly
1 cup warm whipping cream   1 Tbsp. hot water
strawberry halves -OR-   1 Tbsp. Kirsch
   whole raspberries

    Soften cream cheese. In heavy saucepan, beat egg, extra yolk and sugar well. Add flour and pinch of salt. Blend. Add cream cheese, vanilla, and almond extract, blending until creamy. (NO LUMPS) Put on burner of medium-low heat, and add warm whipping cream slowly, stirring constantly. Cook until thick, stirring constantly with whisk. Cool. When cold, divide between tart shells. Arrange drained strawberry halves or whole raspberries on top of custard and cover with glaze.

    To make glaze, combine jelly and water in saucepan and heat, stirring occasionally until it begins to froth and thicken. Remove from heat, stir in kirsch and let cool just a bit. Pour over tarts to seal the tops. Serve tarts at room temperature or cold after refrigerating.

Robin Lightner

Three Layer Raisin Pie

This is an extra special good raisin pie!!

Average   Preparation Time: 30 minutes
Yield: One 9" pie   Chill: 2 to 3 hours

1 cup raisins   1 cup whipping cream
1 cup sugar   1 cup dairy sour cream
½ tsp cinnamon   2 eggs
¼ tsp. salt   ¼ tsp. cloves
1 3-oz. pkg. cream cheese,   1 Tbsp. butter
   softened   1 baked 9" pie shell
½ cup sifted powdered sugar

Chop raisins, add sour cream, sugar, eggs, spices, and salt. Bring to boil, then cook over reduced heat until thickened, stirring constantly. Add butter; cool completely. Blend cream cheese and powdered sugar together. Whip cream and fold into cheese mixture. Spread half of the cheese mixture into a baked 9" pie shell. Add the raisin mixture and then top with remaining cheese combination. Chill a few hours before serving.

Frieda B. Chase

Vinegar Pie

Average   Preparation Time: 30 minutes
                                 Baking Time: 20 minutes
Yield: One 9" pie   Oven Temperature: 325°

1 baked pie shell   3 eggs, separated
2 cups boiling water   1 tsp. lemon extract
¼ cup vinegar   ⅓ tsp. salt
1 cup sugar   3 Tbsp. sugar
3 Tbsp. flour

Beat egg yolks until thick. Add 1 cup sugar, flour and salt. Mix thoroughly. Add boiling water slowly, stirring constantly. Add vinegar. Cook over hot water until thick and smooth stirring constantly. Add salt and lemon extract. Pour into baked pastry shell. Cover with a meringue made of the 3 egg whites and 3 Tbsp. sugar. Bake in a slow oven (325º) for 20 minutes.

Nubs Wort

Sour Cream Raisin Pie

This is quite rich, but it's prettier with a spoonful of whipped cream on top!!!

Easy
Yield: 1 pie

Preparation Time: 20 minutes
Chilling Time: 1 hour

1½ cups raisins
¾ cup sugar
1/8 tsp. salt
baked pie shell

1¼ cups sour cream
2½ Tbsp. cornstarch
2 eggs

Cook raisins and sugar in water to cover until water is almost all evaporated. Add salt, cornstarch, and sour cream and cook until thick. Add slightly beaten eggs. Pour into a 9-inch baked pie shell.

Mary Mead

Strawberry Pie

Average
Yield: One 9" pie

Preparation Time: 30 minutes

3 pints strawberries
½ cup water
1 cup sugar
3 Tbsp. cornstarch

1 single crust baked pie shell
1 Tbsp. butter
red food coloring

Mash 1 box strawberries. Cook with sugar, water and cornstarch until thickened. Remove from heat. Stir in 1 Tbsp. butter and food coloring. Place remaining berries (whole) in pie shell, pour thickened mixture over. Cool, and serve with fresh whipped cream.

Sandy Bommer

COOKIES AND CANDIES
Aunt Stella's Ice Box Cookies

*This recipe is over 100 years old. It makes a lot of cookies!!!
Cut recipe in half if you wish.*

Easy

Yield: 12 dozen

Preparation Time: 25 minutes
Chilling Time: Overnight
Baking Time: 8 to 10 minutes
Oven Temperature: 375°

1 cup brown sugar
1½ cups fat, -OR- ¾ cup butter
  or oleo and ¾ cup Crisco
3 eggs
1 tsp. vanilla
1 cup nuts, chopped

1 cup white sugar
salt to taste
1 tsp. cinnamon
½ tsp. orange extract
4 cups flour

    Beat sugars and shortenings together. Add beaten eggs.
Blend in flour, salt, and cinnamon. Add flavorings and chopped
nuts. Divide into two long rolls. Place in a long narrow pan, and
put in icebox overnight. Cut into very thin slices and place on
an ungreased cookie sheet. Bake at 350° to 375° for 8 to 10
minutes. They will keep in a covered cookie jar for a long time.

Mildred L. Buchenroth

167

Chris's Sugar Cookies

They are great cookies!!

Average

Yield: 3 dozen

Preparation Time: 30 minutes
Refrigeration Time: 2 hours
Baking Time: 10 to 12 minutes
Oven Temperature: 375°

2 sticks butter
1 cup Crisco oil
1 cup granulated sugar
1 cup powdered sugar
2 eggs

4 cups flour
1 tsp. soda
1 tsp. salt
1 tsp. cream of tartar
1 tsp. vanilla

Cream butter, oil with sugars; add two eggs and mix well. Stir in flour and soda, salt, cream of tartar. Mix well and add vanilla. Mix well. Set in refrigerator for at least two hours. Remove and form balls about walnut size. Place on ungreased cookie sheet and bake in preheated 375° oven for 10 to 12 minutes. The balls may be rolled in sugar, prior to baking.

Jane Skeoch

Easy Almond Bars

Delicious!!!
Easy

Yield: 3 dozen

Preparation Time: 15 minutes
Baking Time: 30 to 35 minutes
Oven Temperature: 350°

2 cups flour
2 cups sugar
1 cup margarine, melted
4 eggs
½ tsp. baking powder

2 tsp. almond extract
pinch of salt
1 Tbsp. sugar
½ cup sliced almonds

Preheat oven to 350°. Gease a 9 x 13" pan. Combine flour, sugar, margarine, eggs, baking powder, almond extract, and salt. Pour into pan. Sprinkle with sugar and almonds. Bake for 30 to 35 minutes.

Barbara Van Genderen

Crisp Oatmeal Cookies

These make good dunkers with a glass of milk!!

Easy

Yield: 6 dozen

Preparation Time: 30 minutes
Chilling Time: 1 hour
Baking Time: 8 to 10 minutes

1 cup white sugar
1 cup brown sugar
1 cup shortening -OR- 2 sticks
   of margarine
1½ cups flour
3 cups oatmeal

2 eggs
1 tsp. vanilla
1 tsp. salt
1 tsp. soda
1 cup nuts, chopped
1 cup chocolate chips

Mix in mixer or by hand. Beat shortening and sugars together, add eggs and vanilla. Blend in the flour, salt and soda. Add oatmeal and cream together. Stir in the nuts and chocolate chips by hand. Form in long rolls on waxed paper and chill in refrigerator for one hour. When ready to bake, heat oven to 325⁰ and slice the dough into ¼ inch slices. Place on ungreased cookie sheets and bake 8 to 10 minutes. Space with room for quite a bit of spreading when placing on cookie sheet. The dough tastes almost as good as the baked cookies. . .

Roberta Richardson

Gran's Peanut Butter Cookies

Very good, excellent for small children to prepare.

Easy

Yield: 3 dozen

Preparation Time: 5 minutes
Cooking Time: 8 to 10 minutes
Oven Temperature: 350°

1 well beaten egg
1 cup peanut butter

2 cups of sugar

Mix well, drop by the teaspoon on greased baking pan or shape into small balls and place on a baking sheet.

Sue Everett

Nut Rolls

Average   *Preparation Time: 3 hours*
                             Baking Time: 20 to 25 minutes
Yield: 90 rolls   *Oven Temperature: 375° to 400°*

1 lb. walnuts, ground fine	2 Tbsp. sugar
2½ cups sugar	6½ cups flour
1 cup water	½ tsp. salt
2 tsp. vanilla	1 tsp. vanilla
1 cup milk, lukewarm	7 egg yolks, well beaten
1 pkg. dry yeast	1 lb. softened butter

Mix walnuts, sugar (2½ cups), water and 2 tsp. vanilla. Cook over low heat until thick. Dissolve yeast in the warm milk and 2 tsp. sugar. Add ½ cup flour to the yeast when it is dissolved.

Work together like pie dough the following: 6 cups flour, ½ tsp. salt, and the butter.

Add egg yolks and 1 tsp. vanilla to yeast sponge and add the mixture to the dough. Mix well with your hands. Take a piece of dough (the size of a walnut) and roll thin. Place tsp. of filling on dough, and roll like a jelly roll. Pinch ends of roll. Continue with the rest of the dough. Brush each roll with egg white and shape into a crescent. Place on greased cookie sheet. Bake in a 375° to 400° oven for 20 to 25 minutes.

Jeanie Staehr

Overnight Cookies

Easy to make and light as a cloud.

Easy   *Preparation Time: 15 minutes*
                                            Baking Time: Overnight
Yield: 5 dozen   *Oven Temperature: 350°*

2 egg whites   1 tsp. vanilla
pinch of salt   ¼ tsp. almond extract
¼ tsp. cream of tartar   1 cup pecans, chopped
⅔ cup sugar   ¾ cup chocolate chips

Beat egg whites until frothy. Add salt and cream of tartar. Beat until they are stiff but not dry. Gradually add sugar and continue beating until very shiny and stiff. Add vanilla and almond extract. Fold in pecans and chocolate chips. Drop by teaspoon onto greased cookie sheets. Place in preheated 350° oven. Immediately turn off heat and leave until morning. Do not open the oven. These cookies bake on retained heat. Keep cookies in airtight container (that is, if you have any left over!!!)

Mildred Buchenroth

Honey Popcorn Balls

Average   *Preparation Time: 1 hour*
Yield: 3 to 4 quarts

3 to 4 quarts of popcorn   1 tsp. salt
1½ cups sugar   2 Tbsp. butter
½ cup honey   1 tsp. vanilla

Combine sugar, honey, and salt. Heat until sugar dissolves. Add butter and vanilla and boil to "hard ball." Mix syrup and popcorn together and form into balls.

Jennifer Clarke

Pumpkin Bars

Average

Yield: 3 dozen bars

Preparation Time: 30 minutes
Baking Time: 25 to 30 minutes
Oven Temperature: 350°

4 eggs
1⅔ cup sugar
1 cup oil
1 16-oz. can pumpkin
2 cups flour
1 tsp. baking powder
2 tsp. cinnamon
1 tsp. salt

1 tsp. baking soda

FROSTING:
1 3-oz. pkg. cream cheese
½ cup butter
1 tsp. vanilla
2 cups powdered sugar

Beat egg, sugar, oil and pumpkin until light and fluffy. Add dry ingredients and mix thoroughly. Spread batter in an ungreased 15 x 10 x 1" pan. Bake at 350° for 25 to 30 minutes.

FROSTING:
Cream together cream cheese and butter. Stir in vanilla, add powdered sugar a little at a time, beating well until mixture is smooth.

Judy Montgomery

D & C's Favorite Fudge

Smooth, creamy and rich!!!

Average
Yield: 6 dozen pieces

Preparation Time: 20 minutes
Chilling Time: 1 hour or more

1 can evaporated milk
3½ cups sugar
4 oz. marshmallow cream
½ stick margarine or butter
pinch of salt

1 12-oz. bag of chocolate chips
4 oz. baking chocolate, shaved,
   chopped, or grated
2 tsp. vanilla

Put the milk, sugar, marshmallow cream, butter and salt into a three or four quart saucepan. Bring to a boil and continue cooking at a full boil for seven minutes. You must stir this concoction continuously throughout the boiling process. I use a wooden spoon with a flat end. It scrapes the pan bottom with a wide swath and prevents the sugar from burning.

Put the chocolate chips and the shaved baking chocolate in a large bowl. Pour the boiling sugar mixture over the chocolate and beat until all the chocolate pieces are melted and the mixture is cooled down to hot. Add the vanilla and beat some more. Pour into a buttered 8 x 12 x 13" pan. Cool and refrigerate. Cut into cubes when cool and set.

Carole Travis

Schoolhouse Ranger Cookies

Easy

Preparation Time: 15 minutes
Baking Time: 8 to 10 minutes

1 cup butter
1 cup sugar
1 cup brown sugar, packed
2 eggs, beaten
2 cups sifted flour
½ tsp. baking powder

½ tsp. salt
1 tsp. soda
1 tsp. vanilla
2 cups rolled oats
2 cups corn flakes
½ cup coconut
½ cup walnuts, chopped

Cream butter and sugar. Beat in eggs. Sift flour with baking soda, baking powder, and salt. Blend into creamed mixture. Add vanilla, cereals, coconut, and nuts. Drop on cookie sheet. These spread to about 4 inches in diameter. Bake at 350⁰.

Susie Carlson

Date Nut Coconut Loaf

A rich and tasty loaf for Christmas. It improves with age and is to be cut like a fruit cake.

Easy
Yield: One 8 x 8 square pan or
one 8 x 3 loaf pan

Preparation Time: 15 minutes
Baking Time: 1 to 1½ hours
Oven Temperature: 250°

1 pkg. of dates
1 cup chopped nuts

1 can Eagle Brand Condensed Milk
1 7-oz. pkg. coconut

Combine ingredients. Line loaf pan with well-greased heavy brown paper. Bake approximately 1 to 1½ hours at 250⁰. Remove brown paper while still hot. After it has cooled, keep wrapped to retain the moisture.

Avis Ranck

APRES SKI

APRES SKI

In Jackson Hole we are blessed with some of the best skiing in the world. Within 20 miles are three ski resorts providing excellent skiing from novice to super expert. Because of this and because Jacksonites are just plain outdoorsy Apres Ski or Apres anything has become a tradition in Jackson Hole country. And to go along with "Apres" what better than Fondue. Fondue isn't just a dinner, it's an event with everyone participating and making a fun party. So, what better on a cold winters night. Invite the neighbors over or friends off the slopes and have a "Fondue Party."

Hot Buttered Rum

This keeps beautifully in freezer, and is absolutely heavenly.

Easy
Yield: 1½ quarts

Preparation Time: 10 minutes

1 quart vanilla ice cream
1 lb. brown sugar
1 tsp. nutmeg

1 lb. powdered sugar
1 lb. butter
1 tsp. cinnamon

Have butter at room temperature. Cream butter and sugar together, then add nutmeg and cinnamon. Add ice cream to mixture and put in cartons and freeze.

To Serve: 1 to 2 tsp. of topping
1 jigger of rum
fill cup or mug with hot water

Then, just ENJOY.

Jeanne Houfek
Sandy Bommer

Fireside Wine

Easy   *Preparation Time: 10 minutes*
Serves: 6   *Cooking Time: 20 minutes*

3 Tbsp. sugar   2 cinnamon sticks, broken
1 cup water   1 bottle dry red wine
5 whole cloves   nutmeg
1 lemon, sliced thin

Combine sugar, water, cloves, and cinnamon in pan. Cook over medium heat stirring to dissolve sugar. Add lemon and wine. Simmer ten minutes. Serve in mugs with a sprinkling of nutmeg.

Cookbook Committee

Hot Spiced Wine

Easy   *Preparation Time: 10 minutes*
Serves: 6   *Cooking Time: 20 minutes*

2 fifths of red wine   3 cloves
3 apples, peeled and sliced   ¼ cup sugar
2 tsp. cinnamon   1 tsp. lemon juice

Combine all ingredients in pan. Bring to boil and cook over low heat for twenty minutes. Strain and serve in mug.

Cookbook Committee

Hot Toddy

Easy   *Preparation Time: 5 minutes*
Serves: 1

1½ jiggers of bourbon   1 cinnamon stick
1 tsp. sugar   boiling water
2 cloves   nutmeg

Heat bourbon. Place sugar, cloves and cinnamon in mug. Pour warm bourbon in mug. Stir. Heat three jiggers of water to boiling. Add to bourbon. Stir and sprinkle with nutmeg.

Cookbook Committee

Sandy's Cheese Fondue

My friend Sandy is a vegetarian and tried many recipes before she found this one. We all think it's great.

Easy   *Preparation Time: 20 minutes*

½ lb. Swiss cheese, cubed   ½ cup white wine
½ lb. mozzarella cheese, cubed   ½ lb. mushrooms, sliced
1½ Tbsp. flour

In fondue pot or chafing dish, combine flour and wine, bring to simmer and add mushrooms and cheeses. When cheeses have melted and mixture is bubbly, bring to table and keep warm over low flame.

Judy Montgomery

Sausage Balls

Easy   *Preparation Time: 15 minutes*
Yield: 20 dozen   *Cooking Time: 20 minutes*

1 lb. bulk pork sausage   3 5-oz. jars Old English Process
2 cups flour   Cheese
paprika

Mix all ingredients. Shape into small balls. Bake at 325° for 20 minutes.

You can substitute grated Cheddar cheese or cream cheese for Old English.

Robin Lightner

Fondue Bourguignonne

Easy   *Preparation Time: 15 minutes*
Serves: 4

2 lbs. beef, cubed   3 to 5 dipping sauces
oil   salt and pepper

Trim all fat from meat and cut into bite-size pieces. Heat oil in pan on top of stove. Fill fondue pot with oil. Place pot in center of table. Each guest spears a cube of meat and cooks it to his liking. Meat may be seasoned with salt and pepper and dipped in sauces.

Comments: Other meats to do fondue with are chicken cubed and soaked in Teriyaki Marinade. Lamb cubed, chicken livers, shrimp, lobster, pork or a combination for a mixed grill.

Cookbook Committee

Please Note: A fondue pot must be very stable. Wide at the base and narrow at the top. This helps keep it from tipping and from splatter. Heat the oil on top of the stove before putting it on the burner. Recommended temperature is about 375 degrees. Use a good quality of oil, such as Peanut Oil. Wild game marinated in Pinedale Marinade for Game (Wild Game Section) can be substituted for beef.

BLENDER BEARNAISE SAUCE:

Easy   *Preparation Time: 10 minutes*
Yield: 1 cup

2 Tbsp. white wine   1 tsp. dried tarragon
1 Tbsp. tarragon vinegar   ¼ tsp. pepper
2 tsp. chopped green onion

Cook the above over high heat until almost all liquid has evaporated. Pour the mixture into ¾ cup hollandaise sauce and put into blender. Blend for a few seconds.

Robin Lightner

CHUTNEY SAUCE:

Easy
Yield: ¾ cup

Preparation Time: 5 minutes

¾ cup sour cream
¼ cup chutney

pinch curry powder

Combine all ingredients.

Cookbook Committee

CURRY MAYONNAISE:

Easy
Yield: 1 cup

Preparation Time: 5 minutes

½ cup mayonnaise
½ cup sour cream

1 tsp. lemon juice
1 or 2 tsp. curry powder

Combine all ingredients.

Cookbook Committee

MUSTARD SAUCE:

Easy
Yield: 1 cup

Preparation Time: 5 minutes

1 cup sour cream
3 Tbsp. prepared mustard

2 Tbsp. chopped green onions
salt and pepper to taste

Combine all ingredients.

Cookbook Committee

ROQUEFORT BUTTER:

Easy
Yield: ¾ cup

Preparation Time: 5 minutes

4 oz. Roquefort cheese
½ cup butter

1 Tbsp. prepared mustard
1 clove garlic, crushed

Combine all ingredients.

Cookbook Committee

Steak Diane

Average
Serves: 4 to 6

Preparation Time: 10 minutes
Cooking Time: 10 minutes

2 2-lb boneless sirloin tip steaks
2 Tbsp. olive oil
1 tsp. salt
1 tsp. pepper
¼ cup butter

2 Tbsp. cooking oil
2 tsp. dry mustard
1 Tbsp. Worcestershire Sauce
2 tsp. lemon juice
2 Tbsp. parsley
2 Tbsp. sliced, green onion

Place steaks between wax paper and pound to ½ inch thickness. Sprinkle olive oil on both sides of steaks and pepper generously. In large skillet, saute onions and mustard in 2 Tbsp. of butter and cooking oil for 1 minute. Cook steaks in this for 2 minutes on each side, spooning juices once. Salt cooked meat to taste. Put on platter and keep warm. Add 2 Tbsp. butter, Worcestershire Sauce, and lemon juice to juices. Heat and pour over steaks. Sprinkle with parsley and serve with wild rice.

Robin Lightner

Asparagus Spears Parmesan

Easy
Serves: 4

Preparation Time: 10 minutes
Cooking Time: 30 minutes

24 fresh asparagus spears
¼ cup butter

1 tsp. lemon juice
Parmesan cheese

Wash asparagus spears and cut off tough ends. Par boil 5 minutes. Place in oven-proof dish. Melt butter and add lemon juice. Pour over spears. Sprinkle Parmesan cheese over spears and bake at 350 degrees for 30 minutes.

Robin Lightner

Coq Au Vin

Plan an Apres Ski Party the day before and come in from the slopes and pop in oven. Quick gourmet dinner for four skiers.

Average

Serves: 4

Preparation Time: 1 hour
Chilling Time: 1 day
Cooking Time: 1½ hours
Oven Temperature: 400°

1 chicken, cut into pieces
6 slices bacon, diced
2 Tbsp. butter
8 whole mushrooms
8 small white onions, peeled
⅔ cup sliced green onions
1 clove garlic, crushed
2½ Tbsp. flour

1 tsp. salt
¼ tsp. thyme
1/8 tsp. pepper
2 cups Burgundy wine
1 cup chicken broth
8 small new potatoes
chopped parsley

Wash chicken and dry. In Dutch oven saute bacon until crisp. Remove. Add butter to drippings and brown chicken well in it. Remove. Pour off all but two tablespoons of fat and add mushrooms and onions. When brown, remove. Add green onion and garlic and saute for two minutes. Remove. Stir in flour, salt, thyme, and pepper, stirring constantly until flour is brown. Gradually stir in wine and broth. Bring to a boil, stirring, then remove from heat. Stir in all ingredients that have already been browned. Cool and refrigerate, covered overnight. Next day, preheat oven to 400° and add potatoes and bake covered about 1½ hours or until chicken and potatoes are tender. Garnish with parsley and serve.

Robin Lightner

Pineapple in Carmel Kirsch

Average
Serves: 2

Preparation Time: 20 minutes

1 can of pineapple rings (8½ oz.)
1 Tbsp. butter
2 Tbsp. sugar

2 tsp. kirsch
2 scoops of vanilla ice cream

Add 1 Tbsp. sugar to foaming hot butter in skillet. Drain and add pineapple rings. Sprinkle pineapple with remaining 1 Tbsp. sugar. Cook over medium-high heat turning pineapple rings until golden brown and sugar carmelized. Add kirsch to pan. Touch with lighted match to flame kirsch. (Cooking time less than 5 minutes.) Serve hot on dessert plates with scoop of ice cream.

Rosemary Laumeyer

Chocolate Pots De Creme

Easy   *Preparation Time: 5 minutes*
Serves: 4 to 6   *Chilling Time: 1 hour*

1 6-oz. pkg. semi-sweet chocolate   1 tsp. vanilla
   chips   2 tsp. dark rum -OR-
2 Tbsp. sugar   1 tsp. instant coffee
pinch salt   ¾ cup hot milk
1 egg

In blender put first 6 ingredients. Heat milk and pour over ingredients. Cover and blend about one minute. Pour into custard cups or chocolate pots. Chill at least one hour. Serve with a dollop of whipped cream.

Robin Lightner

Dessert Fondue

Easy   *Preparation Time: 15 minutes*

1 angel food cake   9-oz. Swiss chocolate, broken
fruit (bananas, pineapple,   in pieces
   strawberries, etc.)   ½ cup whipping cream

Combine cream and chocolate in pot. Stir over very low flame until melted and mixture is smooth. Arrange cake pieces and fruit on platter and let each guest spear and dip their own.

Robin Lightner

Loopy's Peaches

Easy   *Preparation Time: 10 minutes*
Serves: 6   *Cooking Time: 20 minutes*

12 can peach halves   ½ cup rum
1 cup brown sugar   vanilla ice cream
1 tsp. cinnamon   whipping cream
½ cup chopped nuts (pecans,
    almonds, or walnuts)

   Place peach halves in oven-proof pan. Mix sugar, cinnamon and nuts together. Sprinkle over peaches. Pour rum over peaches and bake 20 minutes at 350 degrees. Meanwhile, whip cream. To serve put two peach halves and some juice into dish. Top with generous scoop of ice cream and whipped cream.

Rosemary Laumeyer

Index

"THE HOLE THING" Vol. I
Favorite Recipes of Jackson Hole
St. John's Hospital Auxiliary, P. O. Box 428
Jackson, Wyoming 83001

Please send me____copies of *The Hole Thing Vol. I* at $10.95 per book
        Wyoming residents add 5% sales tax   .55 per book
        Handling charges   2.50 per book
Enclosed is my check or money order for $_____
Name_____
Street_____
City_____State_____Zip_____
   Make checks payable to St. John's Hospital Auxiliary Cookbook
       Prices subject to change without notice.

— —

"THE HOLE THING" Vol. I
Favorite Recipes of Jackson Hole
St. John's Hospital Auxiliary, P. O. Box 428
Jackson, Wyoming 83001

Please send me____copies of *The Hole Thing Vol. I* at $10.95 per book
        Wyoming residents add 5% sales tax   .55 per book
        Handling charges   2.50 per book
Enclosed is my check or money order for $_____
Name_____
Street_____
City_____State_____Zip_____
   Make checks payable to St. John's Hospital Auxiliary Cookbook
       Prices subject to change without notice.

— —

"THE HOLE THING" Vol. I
Favorite Recipes of Jackson Hole
St. John's Hospital Auxiliary, P. O. Box 428
Jackson, Wyoming 83001

Please send me____copies of *The Hole Thing Vol. I* at $10.95 per book
        Wyoming residents add 5% sales tax   .55 per book
        Handling charges   2.50 per book
Enclosed is my check or money order for $_____
Name_____
Street_____
City_____State_____Zip_____
   Make checks payable to St. John's Hospital Auxiliary Cookbook
       Prices subject to change without notice.